Adaptability
The art of winning in an age of uncertainty

Adaptability
The art of winning in an age of uncertainty

MAX McKEOWN

KoganPage

LONDON PHILADELPHIA NEW DELHI

First published in Great Britain and the United States in 2012 by Kogan Page Limited

120 Pentonville Road	1518 Walnut Street, Suite 1100	4737/23 Ansari Road
London N1 9JN	Philadelphia PA 19102	Daryaganj
United Kingdom	USA	New Delhi 110002
www.koganpage.com		India

© Max McKeown, 2012

The right of Max McKeown to be identified as the author of this work has been asserted by him in accordance with the Copyright, Designs and Patents Act 1988.

ISBN   978 0 7494 6524 7
E-ISBN   978 0 7494 6460 8

British Library Cataloguing-in-Publication Data

A CIP record for this book is available from the British Library.

Library of Congress Cataloging-in-Publication Data

McKeown, Max.
    Adaptability : the art of winning in an age of uncertainty / Max McKeown. – 1st ed.
        p. cm.
    Includes bibliographical references and index.
    ISBN 978-0-7494-6524-7 – ISBN 978-0-7494-6460-8   1. Adaptability (Psychology)
2. Success.   I. Title.
    BF335.M395 2012
    155.2′4–dc23

2011049245

Typeset by Graphicraft Ltd, Hong Kong
Print production managed by Jellyfish
Printed and bound by CPI Group (UK) Ltd, Croydon, CR0 4YY

Contents

Introduction: In search of adaptability   1

PART ONE   RECOGNIZE THE NEED TO ADAPT   11

Rule 1   Play your own game   13

Rule 2   All failure is failure to adapt   19

Rule 3   Embrace unacceptable wisdom   27

Rule 4   F*** with the rules   39

Rule 5   Stability is a dangerous illusion   51

Rule 6   Stupid survives until smart succeeds   69

PART TWO   UNDERSTAND NECESSARY ADAPTATION   79

Rule 7   Learning fast better than failing fast   81

Rule 8   Plan B matters most   89

Rule 9   Free radicals   101

Rule 10   Think better together   111

Rule 11   Get a kick-ass partner   125

PART THREE   ADAPT AS NECESSARY   133

Rule 12   Never grow up   135

Rule 13   Hierarchy is fossil fuel   141

Rule 14   Keep the ball   147

Rule 15   Swerve and swarm   153

Rule 16 Get your ambition on   167

Rule 17 Always the beginning   181

Final words   193
Acknowledgements   197
References   199

Index   217

Introduction: In search of adaptability

This is a book about how people adapt. It's also a book about winning. Not just winning by playing the same rules, but playing better. And not just winning where there has to be a loser. My interest is in understanding more about how social groups can move beyond the existing rules to find games that allow more people to win more often. New games can make everyone better off than before.

Adapt or die is not the only choice. Our adaptive choices and actions influence what happens to us. Just to maintain things the way they are takes effort. Just to survive can require blood, sweat and tears. Yet surviving is an opportunity; adaptability is more than flexibility, it's more than merely coping with a miserable set of choices in an unhappy game.

In the future, you can try to maintain what you already have, or you can attempt to transcend the constraints of your situation. We're part of a long chain of adaptive moves. Each move has changed the circumstances of our ancestors, until we arrived. Now it's our turn.

Adapt or die is not the only choice. In the future, you can try to maintain what you already have, or you can attempt to transcend the constraints of your situation. We're part of a long chain of adaptive moves. Each move has changed the circumstances of our ancestors, until we arrived.

Now it's our turn. Our adaptive choices and actions influence what happens to us. Just to maintain things the way they are takes effort. Just to survive can require blood, sweat and tears. Yet surviving is an opportunity; adaptability is more than flexibility, it's more than merely coping with a miserable set of choices in an unhappy game.

How do some people start from a losing position and end up winning? How do others follow the reverse path, starting from a winning position and end up losing? Why do individuals, groups, markets and nations end up in situations that are mutually destructive? What can we do to move from miserable equilibrium to joyous disequilibrium? In short, what are the rules of adaptability?

Finding answers to these questions means examining the science of adaptation for clues that would be helpful in developing practical rules.

It also means looking at historical and recent examples to see what patterns, or strategies, of adaptation have worked in the real world full of messy, irrational, self-interested normal people.

Jared Diamond, in his ground-breaking book *Collapse*, suggests that societies may face four similar problems. They may have to struggle with environmental damage, climate change, hostility from enemies, and lack of support from neighbours. Faced with similar threats some fail while others succeed. It is the response that matters, and, since the response is all we can control, it is the response that matters most. Our ability to adapt is what makes the difference.

Culture, science and technology are the primary mechanisms of human adaptation. We can change the way we behave as groups, we can understand more about our world, and we can develop tools that enhance our ability to do almost anything. While far from the gods our ancestors worshipped, we are still the best on earth at changing our circumstances with non-genetic changes to the way we live.

Science studies what is, what was, and what may be. Researchers observe what happens to discover the mechanisms behind what they see. Curiosity drives their search to understand what drives events and actions. There is no single science of adaptability but all scientists seek to understand part of the puzzle of how and why things do or do not change.

In the course of my own research, there was no prejudice against any source of knowledge about my question. In part, that's about my view of the universe, my curiosity, does not set up boundaries between insights gained from observing improvized comedy on late-night television or from detailed measurements of ant colonies. They can all be relevant.

Some strands of scientific enquiry proved to be of particular importance because they include a number of scientists who have asked questions that directly relate to mine. Intriguingly they are often working in isolation from each other. They have asked their questions from within their scientific speciality and do not appear aware of findings from elsewhere. This book brings some of those theories together, across disciplines, for the first time. It combines those discoveries with my own independent insights.

If you want to dig deeper into those academic fields use the additional references at the back of the book. Some of them are fairly technical but I've tried to provide some that are more accessible as a starting point. The question this book asks is valuable; the answers are worth your time and it will be my pleasure to have provided a guide to some of them.

People seek to survive. Most of us want to live well. And many of us want to live as well as possible. We seek advantages but not all of us succeed. Sometimes because we don't know how we want to control circumstances, sometimes because we ignore for some reason what can be done.

Not knowing how can be about individual ignorance, something we don't know that other people do know. It can also be general ignorance in our social group, organization or humanity. It can be something that is not known, some new information or skill that has to be found, discovered, created and made to work. Or, quite often, what can be done is not done.

Adaptations may be deliberate or non-deliberate. They may also be successful or unsuccessful. There are adaptations that lead to failure for the entire social group. There are adaptations that allow the group to survive but leave people in a miserable situation. There are adaptations that improve the group's situation in a desirable way. And there are adaptations that transcend the situation and create a whole new game.

In my exploration of adaptability, there are three steps that have to be followed if there is to be deliberate adaptation that works. There is a lot to know about each step, and they are far from simple to get right. Depending on the nature of the problem or opportunity, they can involve huge amounts of work or very little; centuries to accomplish or minutes.

- **Step 1: Recognize need for adaptation.** If no one recognizes a need or opportunity to adapt there can be no deliberate attempt to adapt. It's possible that someone will accidentally change behaviour in a way that improves the situation, yet this cannot be relied upon. Luck is the best of all tools but even luck is helped by a clear desire to improve something.

- **Step 2: Understand adaptation required.** Recognizing the need for adaptation is a good start, but there are many people, and whole nations, that recognize problems without knowing what to do about them. They worry a lot about the need to make changes. They may want something different but still not know how to get what they want. So they fail.

- **Step 3: Do what is necessary to adapt.** It's entirely possible to know that you should be making changes to solve some problem or grab hold of some great opportunity, without doing anything to change. It's fairly common for people to know what is necessary and still not do what it takes. So that the greatest plans and most urgent needs are never met.

In my research, these three steps explain at a high level what led to successful or unsuccessful adaptation. There's detail and work in each step, and they are not meant to suggest that solving tough problems is always easy. Yet the effort required to cope is not necessarily any greater than the effort to survive, or the effort to cope. The difference is small.

The difference is focus. The difference is difference. You need to be able to imagine various future situations, some worse, some the same and some better. Imagination allows you to recognize a problem while there is still time to solve it. Imagination allows you to move outside the limits of the existing game and figure out how to create new rules.

The outcomes of adaptation, or lack of adaptation, may be collapse, survival, thriving or transcendence:

- **Collapsing** is the end of the social group. The group ceases to function. Everyone may abandon the group as is the case with mass immigration, defection or resignation. The group may lack the resources to support its obligations and be disbanded even without abandonment. This may take the form of bankruptcy, extinction, anarchy or even death.

- **Surviving** is usually better than collapse because the group continues to exist. The problem is that the situation is not desirable; it may even be miserable. The group continues to have resources, it continues to function as a group in various forms but people are not satisfied, growing or improving. They are surviving without prosperity, pride or joy.

- **Thriving** is much better than coping because the group is enjoying success in its current situation. The rewards and benefits of their daily efforts are worthwhile and desirable. If the game demands a loser then those thriving are the winners. If resources permit many winners then thriving involves many enjoying the benefits of a winning game.

- **Transcending** allows escape from the constraints of the existing situation and to rise above it. The players create a new situation and a new game with new rules and improved outcomes over the long term. The group has moved from one way of living or working to a better way. Thriving was good within the old rules, but transcendence allows more for everyone.

These success levels are not fixed. There is overlap between them. The same group may cope in some things, be miserable in other activities, and be thriving at some of what it does. Individuals may be members of different groups and experience failure and success depending on the group.

Each of these terms can be relative. Collapse can be catastrophic involving millions or involve only a small part of a couple of people's lives. Some levels of thriving may be just a bit better than surviving. Some groups may survive in systems delivering prosperity because people have transcended the limitations of miserable systems in the past.

The levels of adaptation success will also change over time with a group moving from coping to thriving and then to transcendence many times, but equally capable of dropping back. Social adaptation is a system with relegation and promotion; it is always the beginning no matter how many times you have failed or succeeded.

Whatever situation you are faced with there will be some level of choice about how you respond. Typically the more time you have the more choices you have but that is not always how it seems. And it's often the case that people delay, for many reasons, making any choice so that the time they thought they had is squandered. Choices can be made that leave you in a worse situation than before, leave you exactly where you were, or with imagination and luck put you in a significantly better situation from then on.

There are no hero companies. There are no perfect leaders. Instead of focusing on just a handful of corporations, we will examine many different stories of how individuals and groups have attempted to adapt. Some of them have failed so completely that their group has ceased to exist; others have succeeded so spectacularly that they have changed history.

We will explore the nature of adaptability, not as a static set of values but as a dynamic set of principles. In particular, we will look at the mechanisms that either leave groups of people stuck doing what they have always done or allow those same people to do something new.

Doing nothing requires effort. Over time, that effort is greater than the effort necessary to improve, or move somewhere better. The trick is to engage sufficient numbers of people in redirecting their energy. This can be done either by convincing them to refocus or by changing the way the social group works so that they refocus without a conscious decision.

From recognition to adaptation

For ease of reading, I've divided the book into three main parts, each focused a little more on a particular step in the adaptability process. This will make it simpler for you to see the way each rule works, although each rule of adaptability will also examine all three of those steps. Luck can remove the necessity of recognizing the need to adapt, and even an understanding of what adaptation is needed, but it cannot remove the requirement for action.

To show how adaptability works, we'll look at a rich set of examples, problems and situations. We'll discover the 15-year-old geneticist working from his basement, and the Italian town that said no to seemingly inevitable change. Along the way, we'll visit the adaptation of Western technology to the social structures of sub-Saharan Africa and explore how quantum games may solve some of the world's trickiest problems.

We will look inside global corporations like Starbucks, Netflix and McDonald's to see how they flirt with extinction, create internal barriers to adaptation, and adapt to transcend their situation. We will investigate some of the most fascinating psychological experiments to understand better the behaviour of social groups and the value of rebellion.

Human attempts to adapt are not restricted to any particular period in history, and such attempts may involve individuals, small groups, large organizations or entire civilizations. The need for improving adaptability can be found everywhere. The consequences of failing to adapt, or adapting in ways that are counterproductive, even miserable, can be seen in the world's great stagnation and seemingly unsolvable crises.

Part of winning in an age of uncertainty is experimentation, trial and error, learning from our mistakes. Yet there is more to adaptability than a willingness to risk failure, there is more than inner confidence. It is entirely possible to fail repeatedly and learn nothing. It is also common for humans to learn lessons that do not lead to changes in behaviour. We may repeat the same mistake over and over again, or may simply avoid the breakthroughs that seem inevitable given the scale of our need.

Events of the past few years have underlined the value in the principles discussed in my previous books. First, it has proved impossible to control the waves of social and technological change. My advice to learn how to surf those waves, reacting intelligently to circumstances, does seem better than relying on plans that are based on simple extensions of the past.

Second, crisis has become a constant in the daily lives of nations, governments, corporations and individuals. When I said crisis was a terrible thing to waste, it was not certain that there would be so much of it to go around. When I explained the difference between disaster, where there is no choice left, and crisis, a critical turning point, it was not known that the next decade would be spent trying to make that turn.

Adaptability is the most important of human characteristics. Survival is opportunity; it's the opportunity to create a better game, a better situation, a better life for us all. But it's not enough. As we explore together over the following pages, hopefully we'll discover ways of learning faster from failure, and adapting beyond the dangerous constraints of existing systems. There are seven billion of us now, so it has never been more important for us to improve our ability to adapt.

All failure is a failure to adapt. All success is successful adaptation. Adaptability is about the powerful difference between adapting to cope and adapting to win. Adaptation is important in all life and so this book will examine examples from business, government, sport, military and wider society to bring the rules of adaptability to life. From the world's most innovative corporations to street-level creativity emerging from the slums. From McDonald's to Sony, from post-war Iraq to the revolutions of the Arab Spring, from the bustling markets of Hong Kong to the rubber-marked circuit of the Monte Carlo Rally.

Human history is a story of adaptive collaboration and between groups and individuals. It has never been more important to understand how to think better and adapt in successful ways to our age of uncertainty. We'll be considering the following questions:

- How do some groups adapt better to uncertainty?
- How can leaders create a culture of super-adaptability?
- How can you transcend the constraints of your situation?

Innovation is important but not enough. Strategy, branding, marketing and operations are all useful, but insufficient. You can't separate circumstance from action when you try to explain success and survival. It's entirely possible to do the right thing according to an outdated playbook. Or to find a new better way of doing something that still leaves people trapped in the miserable equilibrium of an unwanted situation.

You can improve every day of every year and still fail. You may fail to adapt to the specific demands of your situation, a new market you don't even understand or any enemy playing a different game with different rules. Or you can be part of the group that adapts faster and smarter than the situation changes. You can think your way to a better future.

Part

1

Recognize the need to adapt

For the foreseeable future, the future will be unforeseeable. You can be fairly certain that there will be uncertainty. You can be confident that events will overtake your plans, and that the actions of others will require response. And you can be pretty sure that if you don't recognize the need to adapt, then it's difficult to make any changes.

'We didn't adapt fast enough' is a common enough explanation for the poor performance and disastrous leadership of many organizations. It's been used by politicians to explain the opportunities lost through years of war that create more problems than they solve. Adapting too slowly can be damaging or fatal. Not recognizing the need slows adaptation.

'We got it wrong' is less popular but just as relevant. People can move rapidly but in the wrong direction. Groups can act quickly but make the wrong changes, leading to the opposite of what was intended. The ability to recognize the mistake and adjust direction is valuable, not just once but as often as necessary to move towards a more desirable place.

People, particularly in groups, can end up confused about what to do next for the best. People can split up into factions and fight over various flawed route maps. They can also sit complacent about the future because they are unaware of the changes around them, the changes coming. When change arrives that contradicts the experience of the group they may be left in a state of bewilderment, unsure and uncertain.

The true mother of invention is curiosity. We may use the ideas of others because we need them, but new understanding does not arrive simply when needed. If it did, people in tough situations would always find a way to overcome them through ingenuity, but they don't. It is entirely possible for an individual, group or nation to try nothing new in response to enduring responses. Necessity does not guarantee adaptation.

If you're not curious, you have fewer options when a familiar situation changes. As Virginia Rometty, the new CEO of IBM put it, you may be only one mistake from irrelevance. Not if the mistake is small or temporary, but certainly if the mistake changes the direction of the group in a way that compounds the nature of the mistake, then survival may be threatened.

The most successful adaptors are curious. They understand that stability is a dangerous illusion, and reach beyond the limits of what is to what may be, both good and bad. They reach out beyond the obvious questions to non-obvious answers, and are willing to embrace unacceptable wisdom as a way of increasing the options available. They do not simply accept the choices they are given but actively seek better choices. New choices.

Rule

1

Play your own game

If you are getting whipped playing by the existing rules, get used to losing or change the game. If you can't win by standing and fighting then run and hide. If you can't win by being big, be small. If you can't win by being small, be big. The first rule of winning is that there is no one way to win.

The Ancient Greek poets described the monstrous Hydra with more heads than the vase-painters could paint. Worse, for attackers, for each head cut off, the Hydra grew back two more.

The Hydra was eventually defeated by Hercules with the help of his nephew, Iolaus, who stopped the new heads growing by holding a torch to the headless tendons of the neck. It then became simpler to work his way through each of the mortal heads until, with a mighty swing he decapitated the final, immortal head.

This mythical encounter illustrates an ongoing struggle between different approaches to the art of winning. The Hydra seeks to replace heads quicker than they can be destroyed. It attempts to defend its centre at the cost of temporary damage while defeating its enemy by moving rapidly and powerfully. Instead of one giant head, it has nine. Instead of heavy defences, the Hydra substitutes speed.

Any attacker would be initially confused because the behaviour is so unexpected and works against the strength of the attack.

Any seeming success increases the strength of the enemy. It is a strategic adaptation that weakens the side expending the most effort. Physical resources are wasted with every attack while mental reserves are depleted with every renewal.

An example of this hydra problem faced the US strategy, or military doctrine, known as 'shock and awe'. It was formally introduced to the lexicon in 1996 by the National Defense University. Its authors, Harlan Ullman and James Wade, were generous in their praise for both the US military and their ability to achieve rapid dominance:

> It is, of course, clear that U.S. military forces are currently the most capable in the world and are likely to remain so for a long time to come [...] We seek to determine whether and how Shock and Awe can become sufficiently intimidating and compelling factors to force or convince an adversary to accept our will [...] Total mastery achieved at extraordinary speed and across tactical, strategic, and political levels will destroy the will to resist.

Shock and awe became more widely known by the public during the 2003 invasion of Iraq when the term was used by US officials to describe their overarching strategy. The idea was that dropping enough precision bombs would destroy the chain of command and demoralize Iraqi forces, who would then surrender. In turn, ground forces would be warmly welcomed by Iraqi citizens who would form a stable, USA-loving democracy.

On Friday 21 March 2003, the main attack began. More than 1,700 bombing missions were carried out with over 500 using cruise missiles. Two weeks later ground forces seized Baghdad. Three weeks later the USA declared victory. And on 1 May, President George W Bush landed a jet on an aircraft carrier and, under a giant banner, declared 'mission accomplished'.

At first, to some, it seemed shock and awe had worked. On 27 April, *The Washington Post* published an interview with Iraqi soldiers who said they stopped resisting because 'it wasn't a war, it was suicide'. Yet, in truth, resistance had not stopped, it had simply adapted to the impossibility of winning the war by US rules.

Play your winning game is an important adaptability principle. Adapting to win is more than simply coping. You may choose to minimize losses or save face but only as part of a winning adaptation. Surviving becomes one of several moves towards a winning position rather than the game itself.

Over 375,000 soldiers became unemployed on 23 May 2003, following Coalition Provisional Authority Order Number 2 issued by US Administrator of Iraq, Paul Bremer. It was assumed there would be little violent resistance so that a new army of 40,000 new soldiers, trained by US corporations, could replace them – in time.

The traditional stand-and-fight army melted away and became something else, something better adapted to the situation. The insurgency – as it was labelled in the West – was a combination of armed Iraqi citizens, foreign fighters and members of the newly disbanded Iraqi army.

Even worse, action and inaction encouraged the recruitment of new fighters. Actions included deaths of Iraqis as a result of the invasion with estimates ranging from 150,000 to around 600,000, as well as abuses such as those at the Abu Ghraib prison. Even if it is the lower of the two estimates, for a country of 30 million people such a loss did little to inspire support or warmth. Inaction included the damage to infrastructure and institutions that left people unable to build lives or livelihoods.

The following is an illustration from three years after the invasion of the frustration that provides the background to resistance:

> Irritation grows as residents deprived of air conditioning and
> running water three years after the US-led invasion watch the

massive US embassy they call 'George W's palace' rising from the banks of the Tigris. The diplomatic outpost will be visible from space and cover an area that is larger than the Vatican city and big enough to accommodate four Millennium Domes.

Forces of violent resistance were supported by a majority of Iraqis who wanted to be rid of what was seen as an occupying, colonial army. This level of public support further multiplies the motivation of individuals involved in the resistance and increases their effectiveness in resistance.

There were 139 American deaths from the period between the start of the invasion and President Bush declaring 'mission accomplished' and more than 4,335 since that date. The point is not that Iraqi resistance has defeated the US army. The point is that despite huge numbers of Iraqi deaths and over $800 billion spent on the war, the US army has not found a strategy to disarm or defeat the Iraqi resistance.

Multiply to overcome. If the other side of a strategic game decides to disperse, fragment and divide to multiply then it becomes harder to defeat. It's a form of swarming. And in practical terms final victory is denied as long as even one invisible, hard-to-find, motivated player continues to play.

The adaptation of strategy of resistance to US forces was very rapid, as was the disappearance of the official Iraqi army. In contrast, adaptation of the US strategy was excruciatingly, dangerously slow.

The guiding assumptions of the US strategy in Iraq were wrong and this was noticed almost immediately. Yet the US strategy, and accompanying military response, remained stupidly slow. It was clear to some inside and outside the US chain of command that the approach needed to change quickly but it did not. Understanding how the adaptive response was delayed provides valuable insights into what slows down or speeds up adaptability.

One argument put forward is that the USA had to learn how to deal with a new set of problems. The army had to learn on the ground, while being attacked, what it could not learn before it invaded. They had to learn from experimentation what eventually, through repeated trial and error, was a workable strategic adaptation.

As Tim Harford argues, in his excellent book *Adapt*: 'Strategic errors are common in war. This wasn't just about going into Iraq with the wrong strategy. It was a failure – worse, a refusal – to adapt.'

If we want to understand more about adaptability, we want to understand why what was already known was not used more rapidly. We want to know why what was learned was not put into practice. What was delaying the kind of adaptability that would have helped? Why did they refuse to adapt? And what does that tell us about the art of winning?

The US military had already experienced the limitations of decisive force and the unwinnable nature of guerrilla-style resistance. Vietnam provided warnings. Those warnings had been documented, they had been made into movies, they were part of the American cultural heritage.

Likewise, the experience of the USSR in Afghanistan was a bloody case study of resistance and humiliating, costly defeat. The USA was the foreign power who helped – they should have known the potential for failure. Its CIA had provided guidance and training, while its government had seen the deadly effectiveness of small groups of motivated, invisible resistance.

It is true that every situation is different in some way. It is true that even where a situation is similar the people are different and have to learn for themselves the practicalities of lessons already learned. But it is also true that even *after* the ground experience showed them what didn't work, deficiencies stopped them being open to what *might* work.

Estimated time to adapt is the gap between the situation changing and an organization adapting to those changes. Sometimes it is a threat to the way things are that demands corresponding strategic adaptability. Other times, changes present new opportunities that require adaptation before they can be grasped. In both cases, changes must be recognized, nature of change understood, and the changes made in time to engineer a winning scenario.

Time to adapt can be slowed at any stage of necessary learning and action based on new understanding. This delay can be based either on ignorance of the facts, or of what the facts mean. It may also be based on a form of self-interest which ignores what is happening in order to accrue some other benefit. It is entirely possible for self-interest to lead to ignorance and for ignorance to lead to self-interest.

Individuals suffer from ignorance or self-interest which may negatively impact their organizations. Organizations also experience collective denial. Individuals know what is really happening yet are unable to speak the truth *clearly or powerfully enough* to bring the organization to change its chosen strategy or actions.

This disconnection, or gap, between what is happening and what prompts the organization to adapt creates a reality distortion field that slows any attempt at action. If you can't see the problem you can't respond to the problem. If you can't mention the problem, you can't discuss the problem. And while you're failing to adapt, for reasons of tradition, ignorance or self-interest, your opponent's adaptation whether in war, business, or politics, will continue to succeed.

Rule
2
All failure is failure to adapt

In 2011, on the Fortune list of most admired companies, UPS was first among the 10 contenders in the parcel delivery industry. It was given an average score of 7.42 out of 10 for its overall performance while the US Postal Service (USPS) scored only 3.89. In other words, UPS – an American-headquartered delivery service – was considered twice as impressive as the USPS – also an American-headquartered delivery service. What explains the difference?

One argument is that being owned by government stops the USPS from doing a good job. It is difficult to adapt because there are legal obligations to provide what is termed the *universal service obligation*. The agency has to provide everyone, everywhere with a post service at affordable prices whether or not they can provide those services at a profit.

In return, it was granted what was more or less a monopoly at the time it was set up in 1775. The idea was that the USPS would cover their costs because everyone had to use the service. The situation has changed, with competition, but the USPS has not adapted to it. And one reason for this lack of adaptability is that external regulations don't allow adaptation. Another is that two hundred years of history have encouraged a culture that adapted too well to its perceived constraints. Some of this inability to adapt may be enshrined in union behaviour while just as much seems to be found in management and government behaviour.

If you find a system that is failing, then you have also found a system that is failing to adapt. You need to discover, first, what adaptations are needed for the system to succeed. Second, you should understand what has stopped the system from adapting successfully. And third, you should find out how to free the people in the system to make the necessary adaptations.

In practice, the three steps are related. Usually, the people in the system know what is wrong with the system. If you reach out to them they are the fastest way of pinpointing the problems. This approach has the additional benefit of engaging with the people who do the job. The people in management positions may have to make the biggest changes for organizational adaptation to work. Part of that process is placing the responsibility and authority for adapting as close as possible to the work itself.

Leaders who stay in the boardroom cut themselves off from their extremities. They suffer from organizational tourniquets that prevent blood supply and needed oxygen moving effectively around the body. They may have started as rules with a reason, but they eventually become maladaptive blockers whose existence few understand. Even worse, they bring pressures that reduce and damage sensitivity.

Parts of the organization can become misshapen according to the constraints placed around them. They need rehabilitation. They need a mixture of massage, exercise, stretching and loosening of the constraints that stopped people adapting successfully. Instead of just increasing the urgency, people often need greater slack to find new patterns that allow them to think their way to a game that they can win.

Ford was offered the chance to take easy money. In the aftermath of the financial crisis of 2008, the government invited them to consider a government bailout. Despite losses that year of

$14.6 billion it insisted that it did not need the funds. This was the worst loss in its 105-year history, coming only two years after its previous record loss of $12.6 billion in 2006.

The bailout refusal goes back to 2005 when the chairman, Bill Ford, asked his people to figure out a way of getting the company back to long-term profitability. The new kid on the block, Mark Fields, presented his work to the board at the 7 December board meeting. The plan was made public before the end of January 2006.

'The Way Forward' aimed to adapt the company to the demands of its environment. It would stop producing unprofitable and inefficient vehicles, bring production lines together, close down 14 factories and cut over 30,000 jobs. Ford would reduce the size of the company by the 25 per cent reduction in its market share over the previous decade. Ford also would develop cars faster with its new, and grandly named, Global Product Development System (GPDS).

American rivals were making the same kind of cuts. The Ford cutbacks were a survival adaptation. There are too many cars being produced in developed markets. Even automotive addicts have tired of main-lining the same-old-same-old fuel heavy vehicles. Especially when there were better alternatives from companies that adapted early. The new approach to car development was an improvement, but only aimed to bring Ford closer to its Japanese rivals rather than, for example, get beyond them.

Toyota market share doubled over the same time. It had 7.3 per cent of the world market in 1995 which had risen to almost 15 per cent by 2005. The growth was based in part on superior quality. The quality derived from a culture of constant improvement and the Toyota Production System (TPS). The way Toyota did business made it one of the most admired companies in the world. According to its peers, it was the ninth most admired in 2006, third in 2007, fifth in 2008, and third in 2009.

Toyota saw the future in terms of small, incremental, continual adaptations thanks to ultra-engaged workers. But it also saw the big future, a chance to contribute, and an opportunity to do something remarkable. In 1992, brimming full of the confidence of competence it announced the Earth Charter, outlining goals to develop vehicles with the lowest pollution possible. Not just low pollution. Not just the lowest pollution in the industry. Hear the ambition talking. Toyota wanted to compete with possible.

It takes time and a lot of work to change history. Over the next two years, Toyota moved from their paper adaptation to a specific goal of building a car that is hyper efficient while retaining the benefits of a modern car. They wanted to build a proper little green car rather than a curiosity or monstrosity. Their project sponsor, the general manager of engineering, took over as chief engineer of the new car. In 1995, they unveiled their prototype hybrid electric–petrol car at the 31st Tokyo motor show. The team named it in Latin – Prius – because they got there *before* anyone else.

Meanwhile in Detroit City, GM had just started marketing the gas-guzzling pimp mobile, 6,000-pound Hummer sports utility vehicle (SUV). It was the epitome of all that is wasteful with fuel economy of under 10 miles to the gallon. Hummer drivers received five times as many traffic tickets as other drivers while blind spots made parking difficult and dangerous. Not to be outdone, Ford sold the longest and heaviest sports utility vehicle ever made. The Excursion was built for nine passengers, could tow 11,000 pounds, had a 325-horsepower, 7.3-litre turbo-diesel engine that averaged little more than 14 miles per gallon and weighed over 7,000 pounds.

The Detroit Three preferred to keep churning out vehicles that were bigger, heavier and more damaging to the environment than do something better. They ignored trends they knew about. They played a self-defeating game of denial chicken. The year-on-year damage to their market share, erosion of their profit margins, and buying sales through excessive promotions and cheap financing were all put to one side. This was a long emergency. The crash was never going to happen. And if it did, it wasn't going to hurt their leaders.

By 2008, the financial system had crashed, the USA was involved in two unnecessary, costly wars, and the world had entered its great recession. In 2008, in the world's richest economy, GM and Chrysler were forced to go begging cap in hand to Washington DC, the political home of capitalism. With Ford, GM and Chrysler all losing money, the Toyota Prius had sold more than 1 million vehicles. Within just two more years, world-wide sales had reached 2 million vehicles.

The Prius required adaptability *before* the fact. It was a form of pre-emptive creativity. If originality demands that an obvious fact be followed by a non-obvious solution, then it qualifies. Toyota people were able to accept environmental science, laws of economic scarcity and the needs for self-expression among a certain segment of the buying public. And because they noticed this changing pattern they were able to adapt years ahead of their rivals. They were able to make moves at the genetic level of adaptation.

Even after the success of the Prius it was mocked by a certain group of naysayers. For example, US radio broadcaster, Rush Limbaugh, self-described as the 'most dangerous man in America', felt that 'liberals think they're ahead of the game on these things, and they're just suckers'. Even after its success, he went on to suggest Japan was hit by an earthquake and tsunami in 2011 because Mother Nature was angry about the Prius.

Enthusiastic ignorance is a most dangerous behaviour to enlightened adaptation. Individuals and groups can become hugely successful by telling others what they want to hear or what they are willing to believe. Yet nations and organizations are damaged by this type of maladaptation. Believing that anything clever is liberal, science is a conspiracy, sharing is unpatriotic and that knowledge is selling out, these beliefs stop people seeing what is changing and considering how best to create new winning games.

By 2008, Ford's confidence in its own plans had grown high enough to turn down government funds. It did argue that its competitors should receive bailout funds so that the suppliers they all depended on would survive. It had recognized the necessity of deep adaptation before its Detroit competitors, and in 2006 had set up $23.5 billion credit *before* the financial crash. There was also an opportunity to use this advantage to promote Ford as an independent company at a time when this was particularly popular.

Ford's CEO explained that he had taken the original restructuring plan to over 40 banks to get the financing. He asked for much more bank credit than anyone expected to use, and he had made tough decisions without being forced by government. By reacting as soon as possible to patterns of change, he was able to swerve ahead of the curve. He was able to make changes on a timescale that suited Ford, and invest in R&D to accelerate the development of new technologies. This is also pre-emptive adaptation.

In 2010, Ford earned its biggest profit in 10 years, nearly $7 billion. It followed up that accomplishment with its strongest quarter in 13 years, $2.55 billion on revenues of $33 billion.

Sales were up 16 per cent primarily because of strong demand for more fuel-efficient vehicles. Demand that Ford could now supply. It is demand Ford is preparing to encourage with new partnership deals on hybrid trucks and SUVs with Toyota. They will work together which is, in itself, a superior adaptive strategy.

Chatting at the consumer electronics show in 2010, with his 1950s haircut, red tank top, button-down collar and boyish, infectious grin, Ford CEO Alan Mullally could be seen as a kind of geek hero extolling the virtues of cars as portable iPhones. At the 2011 consumer electronics show in Las Vegas, Ford made another surprise appearance to unveil its new all-battery-powered car, the Ford Focus. Instead of launching at the Detroit car show, Ford has transformed its perspective to view its products as part of something bigger than the automotive industry.

This more accurate view of reality was embraced by Toyota, rejected by a section of media commentators, industrialists and politicians, and appears to be the most powerful characteristic of Ford's CEO. This shift in perception, to a more accurate view of reality, particularly at the top, allows the organization to move more rapidly and adapt situations more effectively into winning games.

Rule

3

Embrace unacceptable wisdom

The first thing they always do is bully you. When the Italian government announced that all villages with fewer than 1,000 residents would be forced to merge with nearby villages to save money, they expected compliance. Bureaucrats assume obedience, and if not obedience, then submission.

Mayor Luca Sellari did not see compliance as necessary. Instead, he decided to rebel. He and the village of Filettino declared their independence from Italy. The village printed its own currency, the Fiorito, translated as 'flowered'. According to the mayor, the name alludes to the currency first used in thirteenth-century Florence, the 'florin', and is meant to suggest the way in which the village will flower as a result of its new situation.

The independence movement has announced a new coat of arms with the motto, 'Nec flector, nec frangor' – we will not bow, we will not break. Citizens plan to invite a member of the deposed Italian royal family to become the new Prince of Filettino. They have met with entrepreneurs to establish a national bank of their new principality.

Many small towns were unhappy at the announcement, but only this group of 544 people has attempted to adapt in a non-obvious way. It would have been obvious to complain, or even write letters of protest to government. Yet these would have been anticipated by the bureaucracies who have adapted in such unimaginative ways to the financial crisis.

In part, the non-obvious response was possible because the villagers looked beyond the immediate situation. They looked to the past when Italy was made of many principalities and dukedoms. They looked to San Marino, a landlocked republic of 31,108 citizens and the world's oldest written constitution. They looked to Monaco, Andorra and Lichtenstein, all viable principalities surrounded at all sides by much larger nations with whom they share language, history and tradition. And they looked to the power of social media by creating a website to make their story of interest internationally.

Reversing the obvious adaptation opens up possibilities. Even just speaking the opposite of the prevailing wisdom out loud can create opportunities. Levi Strauss & Co reversed normal operations strategy when they announced their first global water quality deadlines in 1992. Or when they decided to work with environmental groups to move into water reclamation, water efficiency and reuse even in factories owned by the suppliers of suppliers.

In 2007, they went further when they started to look at a full life-cycle assessment of a single pair of 501 jeans. They figured out that over 3,000 litres of water are used from the production of cotton through the manufacturing process to keeping the jeans clean. Nearly half, 45 per cent, of the water is used after they are sold, so Levi's worked with P&G to raise awareness of the benefits of washing in cold water.

The obvious adaptation would be to hide the facts from their customers, or at least to not go looking for inconvenient truths.

The less obvious adaptation to customer and environmental concerns is to find out how much water was used and then advertise that information. The obvious adaptation would make the customer responsible, through a public information campaign, for the water used in the care of the jeans, and then stop. But the less obvious adaptation would be to accept responsibility for water wastage in the production process and then try to do something about it.

Carl Chiara, director of brand concepts and special projects, wasn't happy. He wasn't happy with the acceptable wisdom. He wasn't happy about the arms race in washing processes in jeans manufacturing. He wasn't happy with the three to 10 times each pair of jeans is washed. And he certainly wasn't happy with the 42 litres of water used in the finishing process to give jeans the designer tucks, creases and wear marks. As he explained:

> We went down to the laundry and told them we wanted to do the most incredible finishing you've ever seen, but we didn't want to use any water. And they thought we were crazy because you go to a laundry to use water. But we got really stubborn about it. And we figured it out. We've done some amazing finishes that don't use water. And part of that has come from challenging conventions.

They invented stone washes without stones. They found a way of rinsing with resin instead of with water. And as a result of all the changes made, the water used in the most efficient production processes went down by 96 per cent. They branded their innovation as Water<Less™. They produced over 1.5 million pairs of jeans using the new processes for the spring 2011 collection. And, in partnership with Matt Damon's charity water.org, they invited other manufacturers to copy their ideas, rather than keeping them as a corporate secret. They want to spread the word rather than merely get ahead.

Many innovative solutions came from creating a problem instead of waiting for a problem to solve. This too is unacceptable wisdom. The ability to rebel against the status quo is a valuable human trait. Rebellion can create problems where none existed. It can resist acceptance which, above all, is the enemy of transcendent adaptability. Our rebellious nature fights against constraints, tilts at windmills, stands up when it should lie down, it fights when it should quit. It refuses the will of the crowd. It rejects easy conformity.

If you want better solutions, you need better problems. This is the benefit to social groups of the perpetually dissatisfied, particularly when they are also capable of perpetual motion, or uncompromising resilience. There is a place in adaptability heaven for those people who set their standards above what exists. Their desire to improve what is around them comes from a deep sense of self; it is innate rather than externally imposed. And as a result, cannot be stopped by external opposition or satisfaction.

This was the strength of Chiara; he didn't want all water to be wasted. It had value beyond satisfying his immediate superiors, or accomplishing a particular goal for profitability. He had to propose something that was non-obvious and likely to be unwelcome. He then had to overcome the traditions of those around him, first in the laundry, then in the wider management structure. Resilience is required to establish new wisdom and create modified systems that allow that wisdom to be embraced.

In 1961, Stanley Milgram was curious. He wanted to know whether many of those who murdered millions of Jews could have simply been following orders. While at Yale University he designed a series of psychological studies that would examine the willingness of people to obey an authority figure. Forty men were recruited using newspaper advertisements, to participate in what they were told was an experiment to learn more about memory and learning.

The experimenter, dressed in a white coat and horn-rimmed glasses, led each individual volunteer into a room filled with impressive-looking electrical equipment. The volunteer, who would take the part of 'teacher', was then introduced to a second man, described as another volunteer, who would take the part of the 'learner' in the experiment.

It was explained that the teacher would read a series of paired words to the learner, and then repeat the first word of the pair. If the learner did not respond with the correct word, the teacher would administer a mild electric shock to the learner. The learner would be in an adjacent room, out of sight. He would be strapped to a chair – so that he did not damage the equipment or himself when shocked. The punishments would increase from 'slight shock' at 15 volts to the 'severe shock' at 450 volts. It was explained that the shocks would not harm the learner since amperage was reduced as the volts increased.

As the experiment continued, the learner would deliberately make mistakes. The teacher then administered what he thought were increasing levels of shocks. In the other room, pre-recorded squeals of pain were played for each shock. The actor playing the part of learner would eventually bang on the wall several times, complain about his heart condition and then go quiet.

Faced with the possibility of having injured the learner, many volunteers said they wanted to stop the experiment. But after they were assured they would not be held responsible for their actions, most continued. If the volunteer said he wanted to quit, the experimenter used an ordered series of verbal prompts: Please continue, the experiment requires you to continue, it is absolutely essential you continue, and you have no other choice, you *must* go on. If a volunteer still wished to stop, the experiment was ended.

The results were startling. It was assumed by Milgram's colleagues that only a very small minority would be prepared to inflict the maximum voltage. Yet despite every volunteer expressing concern, 26 out of the 40 continued to the end as a result of the verbal pressure from the authority figure. Horn-rimmed glasses had overcome their deepest moral imperatives. Conformance was stronger than their compassion.

Yet 14 of the 40 had rebelled. In the context of the experiment, the acceptable wisdom was that the shocks were necessary but for each of the 40 volunteers some character trait allowed them to resist. They were not prepared to accept the excuses offered to them by authority, or to abdicate their own personal responsibility. When the experiment was repeated with different groups and in different countries, the majority always conformed but a minority *always* rebelled.

Deviance, difference and rebellion all play important roles in adaptation. Emile Durkheim, the famed French scientist, argued that deviance provides a counterpoint which the majority can use to define their own identity. The rebel is the exception which proves their rule. The rebel is the monster under the bed.

People can even exaggerate these exceptions into threats which can shepherd the majority in directions they would prefer. From acts as dramatic as terrorism to preferences as personal as clothing or sexuality, differences have all been used to group society. We are safe, we are good. They are dangerous, they are bad.

Diversity has innate value beyond providing a threat. Difference guards against the dangers of sameness. It ensures that there are options, that the number of possibilities is increased. It can provide some protection against following one calamitous path without ever considering turning back, or improves the way you travel.

When the mayor of Filettino declares independence he creates problems and opportunities. When the concept director at Levi's demands no water in the laundry, he provokes creativity with his stubbornness. And when rebels from the great activists to the little-known whistle-blowers swim against the tide, they can sometimes reverse it. If something is thought unacceptable, then it will remain impossible. Not all unacceptable is wise, but not all wisdom is immediately accepted.

One reason for the slow acceptance of minority opinions is that majority opinions get an easier ride. If someone presents conclusions that agree with your existing viewpoint then they are unlikely to receive your most demanding critical attention. Studies of influence show that the opinions of rebels, or minority views, receive more scrutiny than majority views. Thus the minority view, particularly if extreme, will often receive more attention but, crucially, less patience than the majority view. Anyone who wants to change the prevailing wisdom on any subject is going to have to work with that human dynamic.

In 2000, the Portuguese government embraced the unacceptable wisdom that drugs misuse was best treated as a health issue, not as a crime. Contributing to their decision were Europe's worst HIV/AIDS situation and highest numbers of heroin addicts. Portugal could have just opted for a zero-tolerance crackdown blended with impotent moral outrage. The European Union administration was applying pressure to do something but that doesn't explain why Portugal opted for originality.

It's the kind of original thinking that when expressed by anyone in public health or law enforcement tends to create little change. The minority with experience can recognize the solutions but seem powerless. It's exactly the kind of opinion that when expressed publicly by a politician is greeted with hysterical criticism from tabloids, shock jocks, and some religious leaders. Evidence is not enough to convince a closed mind.

Prior to the change in the law, more than 50 per cent of those infected with HIV were drug users, with more than 3,000 new infections of HIV among them each year. Only 23,500 were in treatment for their addiction. The objective of the decriminal- ization strategy was to reduce drug abuse and use by redirecting focus to prevention, and increase effectiveness of health-care networks so all needing treatment could receive help.

It all started in 1998 when the seven-person drugs commission recommended decriminalization. It could not recommend legal- ization because of the various international treaties that obligate nations to prohibit drug use. The government council and the commission agreed on the strategy, so there was relatively little political resistance.

The success has made the law change increasingly popular in Portugal. There are 1,000 fewer new infections of HIV. There are more than 10,000 more people receiving treatment. The numbers of drug users, of heroin in particular, and deaths from drug use have fallen while the crime committed to feed drug habits has continued to decrease.

Tellingly, so far the rest of world has failed to fully embrace the source of this improvement. The wisdom of Portugal's drug policy remains unacceptable for many. Political and cultural systems stay maladapted while they are constrained by dogmatic beliefs and fear of voter backlash.

The USA, for example, spent $74 billion in 2010 on turning drug users into convicted criminals, and only $3.6 billion on treating addiction. In the past 40 years, since President Richard Nixon declared a war on drugs, the USA has spent over $1 trillion, or $500 a second, on a failed programme of drug prohibition, law enforcement, foreign military aid and direct military intervention. In 2010, the director of US Drug Control Policy admitted the term is counterproductive but policy in practice has not changed.

In Mexico, there have been over 41,000 deaths since its President Calderón decided to take on the drugs cartels in 2006. While the government claim the majority of these deaths are the result of gang-on-gang crime, it does not lessen the carnage. In just one year, 50 police officers, 19 mayors and over 3,000 completely uninvolved people have been murdered. Calderón knows it is demand for drugs along with poverty that contributes to the strength of organized crime but insists his strategy is working.

Most people assume the majority is probably correct and are afraid of looking stupid, or being isolated, if they adopt a minority viewpoint. This is true for most people *even* if they are aware the evidence does not match the accepted wisdom of their group. The benefits of being accepted are worth the costs of being collectively wrong.

The minority can be persuasive. In a series of group experiments, everyone was shown a series of coloured slides and asked to identify their colour. A minority of actors in the group were asked to deliberately say that blue slides shown to them were 'green'. Despite the truth being obvious, through insistence they managed, some of the time, to convince the rest of the group that they were green. The actors also succeeded in convincing one in three to agree at least once that the blue slides were green.

The scientist responsible for the experiments was Serge Moscovici, a social psychologist born in Romania where, in 1938, he was expelled from high school for being Jewish. He witnessed the 1941 pogrom in Bucharest and was interned in a forced labour camp until freed by the Soviet Red Army. During his time in prison he taught himself French and eventually illegally emigrated to France to escape anti-Semitism from the Red Army Soldiers.

Serge's experiences suggested to him that small groups have power to change history for good or bad. He claimed that diversity of opinions is proof that majority influence is not universally dominant. He argued that most social change comes from individuals or small groups. In his view, persuasive minorities are the source of innovation and change.

Perspectives are competitive. They often need one set of opinions to be set aside to make room for a replacement set. The majority assume the minority is incorrect. When faced with persistence they ask how the minority can be wrong while insisting that they are right. Refusal to adapt to the dominant view creates at least some room for doubt.

Vitalino Canas is the lawyer appointed by the Portuguese government to make the decriminalization objectives successful. When seeking to influence, he distinguishes between the traditional repressive approach and a new multidimensional progressive approach. And he repeats himself – a lot. Here he is speaking in Brazil in 2007:

> America has spent billions on enforcement but it has got nowhere
> [...] It does not make any sense to apply prison sentences or
> stigmatising punishments to these people, and the outside world
> is increasingly realising this. Instead, a set of public health and
> support measures must be applied to dissuade the user from
> consuming drugs in the future. This is the philosophy behind
> the 1999 Portuguese law I was responsible for.

His approach of distinguishing between two kinds of drug policy – old and new – is powerful. The method of underlining what hasn't worked, something the majority can agree on, has to be repeated constantly to make room for people to change their minds. First situations change, then thinking about the situation, and finally adaptation.

Embracing unacceptable wisdom allows us to benefit from better ways of adapting our situations. Non-obvious suggestions can provoke more ideas that lead to improvements beyond expect-ations. Looking to the past, to the future and outside the day-to-day limits of your village, city, profession, corporation or country will increase adaptive options. If you want to learn, listen to the other side of the argument. If you want to be radical, listen to the rebel.

Rule

4

F*** with the rules

Ants create complex societies with simple rules. So do we. The rules
are remarkably important for allowing us to work together effectively.
The 90 per cent of behaviour we share in common is what allows
us to communicate and collaborate; the 10 per cent of difference is
what allows us to adapt or fail, win or lose.

Knowing the rules is valuable; knowing when to break them
is critical to successful adaptability. If you don't know the
rules they can't help you with shortcuts to what is already
known. Rules contain knowledge. Rules are made of experience,
and much of that experience is useful.

Yet rules may also include prejudice or mistaken beliefs.
Behaviours learned in one set of circumstances may be ill-suited
to new challenges. Even when tradition works, human history
suggests a desire to find a better way, and an ability of some to
actually find a better way.

Ants have routines for dealing with the day to day of existence.
To thrive they must also have ways of breaking those routines
when faced with disturbance to their day to day. In the ant
world, some characteristics are better than others at adapting.
Each of the 22,000 ant species have different combinations of
those characteristics. They also adapt on different levels depending on the time available.

If ants only have seconds to adapt, then the adaptation may happen at the individual level. There is no time for other ants to change what they are doing. But if there's a little more time or the teams that work with the ant are very responsive, then they can try to adapt as a group.

If the ants have days or months to adapt they may allocate tasks differently in response to differences in the environment. Each new generation receives a role before being assigned a new role as they get older. These roles can change so that new ants learn new rules for dealing with new situations or with existing situations in better ways.

With yet more time, adaptation can take place at the level of the colony which institutionalizes the new behaviours and roles. There may also be changes in the direction of production and prioritization of reproduction, a form of recruitment, and on-the-job training. Older ants have been observed coaching and mentoring younger ants.

These changes may over seasons spread to other colonies leading to community (market-to-market) changes. And finally over generations there can be genetic changes that include the new ways of behaving and new skills for thriving in the semi-permanent traits of individuals, groups and the organization.

This time-based adaptation is hugely important to the art of winning. You should make it a priority to consider your own efforts over time. How can you get people ready, able and willing to adapt in the very short term? How can an individual pull in colleagues and resources in flexible ways to deal with short- or medium-term threats? And what can you start, or stop, doing that will put you in a better position to win in the longer term?

Everyone needs the responsibility and power to change what is necessary to win according to the game you have agreed to play.

The front-line colleague needs to know when and how to bend the rules to help out a customer. The contract negotiator needs to know how to adapt the deal to what is on offer without exposing the organization to damaging agreements.

Just as important is how you adapt the wider organization in response to short-term adaptations that have succeeded or failed. And how you consider longer-term changes that can take advantage of what is learned in any pattern of threats. This is what the most adaptive organizations do better than the rest. They continually notice what is happening. They actively seek to adapt ahead of the curve and also ahead of trouble. And they figure out ways to treat events not as exceptions but as triggers to develop new, enhanced capabilities. They may even transform into entirely new organizations. Looking at ants, we find different strands of adaptability:

- **The Opportunists:** Some ant species are particularly good at dealing with uncertainty and constant major changes. They keep their colony size small and avoid specialization. If you never know what's going to happen next, then it's better to be ready for anything. These ants reject overspecialization in terms of behaviour, diet, skills or office space. They are open in matters of mating (polygyny) and rooming (polydomy). They are ready to be flexible about who to mate with and where to sleep, including with other colonies.

- **The Climatists:** Some ant species are great at dealing with very, very stressful environments as long as they are stressful in a predictable way. They know things will be hard, cold and difficult so they specialize in ways that will allow the colony to survive. They have created nests that can keep their temperature several degrees higher than the outside world. The size of the colony increases as the climate gets colder and higher in the mountains, so that they can collect enough food to survive the winter.

- **The Competitors:** A third group of ant species win most often in a direct competition with other ants in a relatively predictable environment. They don't have to fight to survive because the situation is good, and instead they fight for dominance with other ant species. The less specialized ants are flexible but don't do as well against the large, aggressive workers of competitors. The collaborative approaches of the opportunists are less effective when their neighbours don't want to coexist.

In the ant world, competitors build huge nests and have specialized elites. They don't roll with the punches; they just discover and consume resources faster than other ant species. One extraordinarily successful species, Pheidole, has two distinct worker groups. Normal workers are normal-sized, easily trained, and do most of the colony's tasks. The soldiers, with disproportionately large heads, do specialized work and defend the nest.

For ants, as for humans, there are trade-offs between different characteristics *and* between the objectives of competition, opportunism and longevity. Whether a characteristic is a strength or weakness depends on the particular situation.

For humans, as for ants, these abilities can be combined in unique ways to win different games. Some human time is spent directly trying to crush the competition while far more time is spent trying to coexist in a more or less self-interested way. For both, it is best to consider rules as a starting point rather than the final word on how to play.

Considering rules as a starting point is exactly what the most successful competitors in motor racing have done. Because the world of motor racing is ultra-competitive, there is constant friction between rules that have to exist to provide intense competition and the competitor's desire to fight, bend or break the rules in order to finish first. Just as with the ants, each member of every team looks for some way of changing the nature of the game, or finding opportunity within or around the traditional way of playing that game.

The name of Formula One (F1), the most popular global motor sport, comes from the set of rules which all competitors agree to keep. The rules include stipulations that an F1 car be no more than 180 cm wide and 95 cm tall, that engines be normally aspirated, four-stroke internal combustion, and that no refuelling is possible during a race. They specify aspects of what drivers can do during a race, how much teams can spend, and even what kind of aerodynamics can or cannot be used.

One F1 team in particular rose to prominence because they were able to adapt more effectively and find creative ways of winning within the rules. Additional rules changes would always benefit them more than their competitors as long as they were able to maintain their adaptability advantage.

In 2004, Ford put its Jaguar F1 racing team up for sale for $1. Part of the decision was about money – it cost them around $500 million – compared to the marketing benefit. And part of the low marketing benefit was a total of *zero success* on the racing track. Over 85 races completed over five years with not one victory, pole position, or fastest lap.

Red Bull stepped up, agreed to invest $400 million over the next three years, and were rewarded with the team's best-ever finish. Their new team principal, Christian Horner, reported to be a second choice, adapted existing resources into something competitive. With the same chassis and engine the team managed to gain more points than in the previous two seasons combined. Their new drivers, a mix of experience and youth, surpassed their recent achievements and even threatened to win podium finishes.

Despite optimism, new Ferrari engines, and newly recruited technical director Adrian Newey fresh from victories at McLaren, the 2006 season started in a disappointing way. Cooling problems, overheating, engines blew up, hydraulics problems, early retirements and finishes with the laggards meant that they finished seventh again.

In many ways this was the start of something special. The cost of deep adaptation was, as with the ant species, time. Flexibility in races is important but deeper changes were being made. The team learned from each race and from the experience of its new technical director.

An important turning point was reached on the demanding streets of Monaco. After an uninspiring first qualifying round, Newey pushed hard to start close to the front. The team pulled off a strategic masterstroke when it rejected the two-fuel-stop approach of other teams and fuelled driver Coulthard's car just once, at lap 29.

Despite collisions and near misses, Coulthard, a previous winner at the circuit, achieved Red Bull's first podium finish. And Christian Horner kept his promise that if his cars finished in the top three he would jump into a swimming pool naked. That he and the team wore Superman insignia to promote the latest movie seemed appropriate.

In 2007 Red Bull benefited from new Renault engines, a newly designed chassis from their technical director, and a new driver, Mark Webber. Again, the season started badly but steadily improved with another podium position. The cars showed increasing speed. The team showed increasing optimism. They continued to strengthen the technical team and finished an impressive fifth in the constructors' championship ahead of Toyota.

The little guys did well, and were praised. Only halfway into the 2008 season with another new chassis but the same drivers, they had equalled their 2007 points total but this time had an awful end to the season scoring just five points in 10 races. They fell back to seventh place by the end of season, almost as if the progress of previous seasons had been lost. Lewis Hamilton won the championship for McLaren by a single point from Ferrari and dominance by the two biggest names in racing seemed likely.

Then something quite different happened. By the end of the 2009 season, Red Bull achieved an incredible second place. Ahead of McLaren, Ferrari, Toyota, BMW and Renault. The team won their first race and achieved another three victories in first *and* second place.

In 2010, with another new chassis while retaining the Renault engine, it became immediately apparent that they had the best-handling car. After mishaps in Bahrain and Australia the team won first and second, moving into third place overall. Six consecutive pole positions followed and a remarkable nine outright victories. By the end of the season, they won both the drivers' *and* the constructors' championship. They had arrived.

Red Bull had moved from a no-hope team sold for $1 in 2005 to the dominant force in racing in just five years. How had this great zero-to-hero adaptation been achieved? It wasn't just the engines; they were shared with Renault who finished fifth. And it wasn't just the drivers, neither of whom had won championships. It was the mix.

There is no single way that adapting to win is achieved. Red Bull made tens of thousands of changes to every aspect of the cars, drivers and engineering team, all following on from the appointment of Christian Horner as new team principal. The winning chassis was the sixth complete redesign by Adrian Newey. Every race, every lap, every change of rules gave new opportunities for adapting better than the competition.

To increase adaptation opportunities, Red Bull invested in two F1 teams. The Italian Team Red Bull (Scuderia Toro Rosso) shared resources including the design team, chassis ideas, and even drivers. The arrangement led to the 'B' Team winning a grand prix before the 'A' team. As a result, the winning driver, Sebastian Vettel, moved over to Red Bull before becoming F1 champion in 2010. The benefits were so great that sharing chassis designs has since been outlawed by new rules. It's not the only thing they did but it's a great illustration of how two teams can be better than one.

To increase opportunities acted upon, Red Bull has the youngest team principal in F1 who understands some of the limitations of traditional hierarchy. He believes in empowering people rather than telling them how to do their jobs. His age – he was 31 when first appointed – is an advantage when working with the youngest-ever world champion and even his older driver is only 34. The team believe in a more relaxed climate than their rivals. And it is this apolitical climate, or culture, that encourages frictionless ingenuity. You go faster when you don't look like you're trying. More opportunities led to adaptation when there are fewer layers between good ideas and testing those ideas in real conditions.

Of course, it's not only his age. It's entirely possible to be young and inflexible. It's also not just about talking about empowerment. It's equally possible to say empowerment, and practise disempowerment, or descend into maladapted chaos in which opportunities are increased but not acted upon. The adaptation principle of increasing opportunities acted upon must be remembered in judging the effectiveness of any particular policy.

Other teams have not so successfully reduced adaptation friction. McLaren, for example, won the drivers' championship in 2008 when Hamilton achieved the necessary fifth place on the final turn of the final lap of the final place. This was not a team who had significantly moved ahead of their rivals through superior adaptation; this was temporary, in the moment, superiority within the scoring system.

Some of McLaren's best people left. David Coulthard, driver, was discarded but Adrian Newey, technical director and considered one of F1's greatest engineers, wanted to leave for several years. He nearly moved to Jaguar, and then finally arrived at Red Bull in February 2006. Some of that was about money; he was rumoured to be paid US$10 million a year, but much of it was about being able to work without constraints.

The differences in management style are deliberate. Christian Horner has made it clear that McLaren's approach is exactly how Red Bull doesn't want to treat their drivers. Instead of tightly controlling their image by insisting they refer to the team correctly, wear the correct merchandise, and appear professional, Red Bull focus on getting their drivers to relax in the cars, with the press, and with each other. The appearance of professionalism can create brittle, superficial behaviour instead of the deep, fluid behaviour necessary for superior long-term adaptation.

Some of McLaren's efforts to alter the rules have been clumsy, as when they attempted to mislead stewards at both the Australian and Malaysian races. Similarly, Renault tried to gain advantage by ordering one of their drivers, Nelson Piquet Jr, to deliberately crash his car during the 2008 Singapore race. This tactic achieved the goal of allowing their other driver, Fernando Alonso, to win the race but their attempts to cheat were discovered and the team was given a two-year suspended ban.

To increase their adaptation advantage, Red Bull actively looks for how rule changes could disproportionately benefit their team's performance. This is a relative adaptation that seeks to exploit what your competitors ignore. These adaptations do what competitors are least or most likely to do (or not do). Given the slack to be creative, the central team of Adrian Newey, Rob Marshall (chief designer) and Peter Prodromou (aerodynamics) worked every angle, every possibility presented by the design rules.

This slack matters. Along with desire to find creative adaptations must be the belief that they have the ability and that there will be the opportunity to make them work. Slack allowed them to go back to find what worked in the past in similar circumstances. What has happened *before* is the source of learning; the wider your historical point of reference the more possibilities can be considered to find your best solution. Effective adaptation does not benefit from a new-new obsession if that blinds your team to other options.

Red Bull has even been accused of overspending by around $60 million. They deny the accusations but whether true or not, the debate suggests the ways in which teams will attempt to adapt. Ferrari suggested that Red Bull have lacked respect deserved by a team that has won 16 championships. But too much respect for rules and traditions established by the dominant player is unlikely to help the newcomer to win.

Games are often won long before they are played in public. It would be in Ferrari's interest to influence the rules of the game to suit them, and to influence the interpretation of those rules to help them. It would also be natural for the game to want its most illustrious member to gain yet more victories. They receive, for example, $80 million more when they win than any other team.

Virgin fought British Airways in the courts to change the game and deliberately make their biggest competitor feel discomforted. It was a clever example of understanding the power of rules to enlist forces more powerful than your competitor. Microsoft has used similar adaptive tactics in recent years to try to slow down Google in the search engine space. Attempts to get antitrust authorities involved may create enough legal noise to distract and potentially disrupt the market leader. The aim is to buy enough time to adapt at a higher level and gain some advantage. Enough time to find the next big thing.

If you are the weaker player, you should understand the rules and deliberately, creatively figure out how to benefit from them. Smaller players can use the law against larger players, or even the conventions that have emerged over time. The alternative is to accept defeat or your place in the game even if unloved, uncomfortable, even miserable.

Rule
5
Stability is
a dangerous illusion

'Our reputation,' the UBS report underlines, 'is our most valuable asset.' 'Our reputation,' the report makes clear, 'is ultimately defined by the actions and decisions we take every day.' And to restore and safeguard 'our reputation', they launched a worldwide brand campaign saying 'We will not rest.'

Little was said about their 65,000 employees other than that there were 65,000 of them. No mention was made of flexibility or adaptability. Nothing was said about uncertainty, chaos or luck. Not one word about the future and what was needed to adapt to demands and shape events. And that was a pity, because in September 2011, one employee lost $2.5 billion.

At first, the CEO, Oswald Grübel, distanced himself from what happened. On the morning of 19 September 2011, he said 'If you ask me whether I feel guilt, then I would say no.' But the fraud took place over three years, the same length of time as Grübel had been in charge. It was part of a pattern of irresponsible trading that had been criticized by the Swiss government, who had bailed it out in 2008, and by its main shareholder, the Singapore government, who had stayed loyal throughout its losses.

Within a week of that rejection of guilt came the CEO's resignation. The chairman, Kaspar Villiger, said that Oswald Grübel wanted to assume responsibility but it felt a lot like the complete opposite. The bank announced that it would be shrinking its investment banking division so that it could permanently reduce its risks. Many shareholders had argued for exactly those changes since the bailouts but it took the fraud to convince UBS that it had no choice but to adapt to circumstance.

The stability at the top of the company seems to have convinced UBS that it could avoid adapting despite what appeared like overwhelming evidence that such changes were necessary. It survived more than $50 billion in toxic debts but did so with strategies more about confidence-boosting denial than situation-transcending adaptation. Grübel came from retirement to try to save UBS before retiring again via resignation.

Back in 2009, Grübel's predecessor, CEO Marcel Rohner, resigned just a few days after speaking of the need to restore 'trust, profitability and stability'. At the time, he argued that the deep institutional experience of UBS would help them restore confidence in the future. Unfortunately, it was exactly those deep, embedded institutional habits that got them into difficulty and those same habits that did not allow them to think their way out of those difficulties. You can't escape bad habits by thinking in old ways. He resisted the changes that were needed because it was too institutionally painful to deliberately cause instability.

In our history, people put up with remarkably awful circumstances. Or, more accurately, people end up stuck in remarkably unhappy situations. Despite efforts to improve the way things are, they stay the same, or even get worse. No one is happy; no one escapes their unhappiness or their dissatisfaction with their part in the wider system.

Each individual move is played to the individual player's advantage. Each person does what seems likely to lead to the best possible result but somehow the sum of all those actions is considered by all as a failure. And this failed game doesn't just happen once, as an unintended consequence of self-interested decisions. It happens again, and again, sometimes for generations with no one quite able to escape the logic of unhappiness.

Typically this miserable equilibrium continues until someone can shift actions past immediate logic towards renewal. It can happen accidentally, with an unplanned event jarring circumstances so that people act quite differently towards each other. It can also happen deliberately, if there is a deep understanding of the game that allows someone to alter the shape and behaviour of the game.

Even where there is a deep understanding of the game, it must exist in the head of someone who is a player in the right position to make some of the necessary moves. There needs to be someone embedded deeply enough in the situation to set off a chain of events. From inside, these events can disrupt the maladapted system. They can transcend the damaging historical patterns that have seemed inescapable.

The area of science that looks most closely at problems of this kind is game theory. It views all relationships and transactions between individuals and groups as a form of game. Not a game that is played for fun, but a relationship that involves moves, or actions, by all players. And a game that leads to outcomes, varying levels of victory and defeat.

The first significant work into game theory began in the 1920s with a series of papers published by Émile Borel. He didn't write much but what he did write was to prove influential. This included his now famous thought experiment about the ability of an infinite number of monkeys to create Shakespeare's complete work if given long enough to keep randomly entering characters into an infinite number of typewriters.

His work had flaws but attracted the attention of others who were inspired to develop it further. Prominent among these was John Von Neumann, a Hungarian-born mathematician. At the age of six, he could tell jokes in classical Greek, by the age of 22 he received his doctorate in mathematics in Budapest, by the end of 1929 he had published 32 major papers, or one per month.

One of those papers was about zero-sum games, where there is a limited amount that can be won or lost, with perfect information, where everyone involved knows what everyone else has done. Von Neumann showed that in such games there is a pair of strategies allowing all players to minimize their maximum losses. These strategies were described as optimal even though real-world results could be mutually damaging and unattractive.

The classic game was the prisoner's dilemma. Two prisoners are kept in separate rooms. Each prisoner has to choose whether to confess and accuse the other prisoner. If both prisoners keep quiet, both receive one year in prison. If one confesses and the other does not, the confessor will be freed while the other prisoner gets 20 years. But if both confess, each will receive five years. The most likely outcome is that both confess unless they have complete trust in the other prisoner, sufficient trust to risk 15 more years locked in a cell while the other man walks free.

From the 1950s, game theory was expanded by many scholars and applied to different kinds of problems in many practical and theoretical fields of study. This ranged from cooperative games, where both groups try to find the best compromise agreement, to non-cooperative games where both groups try to defeat the other.

Not surprisingly game theory in military strategy was given a lot of attention. The attraction was that game theory would provide endless victories to those who understood it best, while dealing countless defeats to those who did not grasp its intricacies. The USA would figure out how to out-think the USSR with the help of genius mathematicians from the old country. Game theory plus nuclear weapons would maintain their superpower status and overcome all enemies.

Yet there were limitations to the power of game theory applied in this way. For one thing, international conflicts are not constant-sum games with a fixed amount to be won or lost. They are variable-sum games where more can be won if all sides make certain choices. Thomas Schelling, an American academic, won his Nobel prize for pointing out over many years, that there can be common interest in cooperating even in games that start non-cooperatively.

Winning is not just about defeating the enemy by killing him or destroying his weapons. Winning is not just about being the last man standing. Or even the last man laughing. Winning can be a game of adaptation: a bargaining process through which all sides may shape a better future.

As Schelling points out, a successful strike by workers is not one that ruins the employer, nor is a successful war one that destroys peace, wealth or the lives of brave young adults. As he argues, the most successful strikes and the most successful wars may be those that never take place. And if that is true of industrial and military conflict, it may be true of many other mutually destructive games in society, business and politics. They are open to the possibility of game-changing games.

There are a number of difficulties with real-world games. There is seldom perfect information available about the choices everyone will make, and so each person must guess what may happen.

They may be wrong about those choices, making inaccurate assumptions about actions and motives. Equally, ability to make choices that actually deliver the best possible outcome may be constrained by prejudice, habit or hatred.

Even where a situation is miserable for all involved, one or all groups may not recognize the possibility of a better situation. Despite recognizing the opportunity for something better they may be unwilling to act because they do not trust or want to help other groups. The rest of the group may be unable to understand what would be necessary to shape a better future or simply unable to break the destructive patterns of behaviour.

If any side is irrational, then rational moves by any other side are made less likely and perhaps dangerous. The hope in a destructive, miserable equilibrium is that somehow the other side can be coaxed, manoeuvred or loved into cooperation. This can be attempted by bribing groups, or threatening groups, making it more attractive not to destroy, but has seldom been enough to overcome the root causes of non-cooperation.

These irrational deadlocks cannot generally be overcome simply by saying that they are irrational. Not only is this taken as insulting, if the accusation is accurate, it cannot be fully understood, accepted, or acted upon precisely because they are irrational. Not necessarily in all matters, but in the particular matter of the miserable equilibrium they cannot see sense. They have at least partial blindness to all strategies based on anything except mutual antipathy and distrust. They refuse better sight.

The Palestinian–Israeli conflict is one of the more famous examples of a game where two groups cannot reach agreement to improve an unhappy situation. Over the past 64 years there have been between 51,000 and 92,000 killings in military actions from both sides.

One estimate for the total cost of the conflict to the global community is $12 trillion in direct support, mainly to Israel, and consequences in terms of increased instability. The same estimate suggests the average Israeli citizen would be now earning nearly twice as much if they had peace.

In 2004, nearly 60 per cent of Israelis and over 50 per cent of Palestinians supported the peace deal put forward by President Clinton in 2000. This Camp David settlement became popular immediately after the death of President Arafat, which led to an increase in optimism and moderation. By 2011, the numbers had dropped to 52 per cent of Israelis and only 40 per cent of Palestinians.

Events since 2004 have decreased the number of supporters for a peace deal. They have either sabotaged themselves in a self-destructive push away from a better situation or been sabotaged by a minority of extremists who do not want a peaceful solution. There have even been accusations that the Israeli government has used formal game theory to avoid peace because an absence of conflict would reduce its influence.

In 2005, Robert Aumann became the eighth person to receive the Nobel Prize in Economic Science for work on game theory. He is a resident of Jerusalem and explains that it is the specific school of thought developed in Israel that provided the basis for his success. It has been argued that use of game theory has prolonged the conflict by deliberately using provocation to destroy the trust necessary to reach a peaceful solution.

Game theory can be as irrational, destructive or limited as any other way of reaching a decision. Starting with the assumption that peace is impossible, for example, introduces prejudice that disallows certain actions. An attempt is made to perpetuate the status quo out of fear of a future that is worse. Yet that fear prevents moves that could make the future better. While the appearance of rationality stops the irrationality of particular actions from being discussed regardless of consequences.

They are beautiful theorems with potentially ugly consequences, a set of strategies deliberately chosen to force the game into vicious infinite regress. These are actions taken by political players who act independently of their own electorate to try to keep everything as it is. It is stability at a terrible price, one that cannot be sustained for ever.

There is suspicion that a two-state solution with endless preconditions is discussed deliberately because it is so easy to sabotage any agreement. Yet, without actual agreement, then a one-state solution with an Arab majority, due to higher birth rates, may be the outcome. And at that point, the architects of prolonged conflict will be forced to choose between democratic equality through reconciliation or risk unwinnable civil war.

Moving beyond the immediate limitations of a miserable game to one played with rules that increase benefits to all groups is possible. But it requires behaviour that is counter-intuitive, particularly to those who have committed to one way of thinking surrounded by those who appear equally fixed in their patterns of behaviour.

Von Neumann showed how easy it was for fairly minor preferences for living among people like us can lead to radically segregated communities. These preferences can grow more dangerous in time as the mutual interests of segregated groups appear to diverge. When it seems natural for one group to prosper at the expense of another's failure, great injustices can happen. Those playing a losing game can be trapped.

'Adapt or die,' Botha declared to white South Africans in 1979. But it would be another 15 years until that adaptation would start to transcend the political past of a damaged society. It would require moves that went beyond immediate rational self-interest to transform the miserable equilibrium into one of the world's most unexpected successes.

South Africa's president recognized the need for adaptation but he wanted to adapt in order to preserve the superiority of whites rather than to change the nature of the game for all.

In South Africa, apartheid trapped a whole country in a specific losing game for more than 45 years. Racial inequality had existed long before but was increasingly supported in law as agricultural reforms and industrialization increased competition for jobs first on the land and then in the cities. In 1905, the right to vote for all black people was removed and they were limited to living in particular areas. In 1910, whites were legally given complete political control over people of all other races. In 1927, blacks were prevented from practising skilled trades.

There were attempts to move away from rigid segregation during the Second World War by the government led by Jan Smut's United Party with support from Indian and mixed-race voters. These reforms were overturned by those who feared that racial integration would allow blacks to compete fairly for jobs and business.

The infamous Sauer Commission claimed that stricter separation of races was necessary to avoid a loss of personality for all groups. In 1948, it formulated laws that divided the country into 13 nations, forcing people to live in those areas defined by race. Identity cards were issued to all over 18 that specified racial group that was determined by official government teams. Marriage or even sex between groups was made illegal. Racial discrimination was established as a requirement for employers.

In 1970, the citizenship of blacks in South Africa was formally removed. Every change was intended to maintain stability of superior political and economic power for the white minority.

It has been argued that apartheid policies adapted according to economic incentives of the majority of white people. When most were workers without capital they supported segregation. As they gained higher-level skills and capital their support switched to an anti-apartheid stance. It had become more attractive to have complementary skills while whites could benefit from a growing newly invigorated economy as its elite.

Such an explanation is informative but doesn't explain why apartheid was so extreme, petty and vindictive. It doesn't make it much clearer why apartheid lasted long after it was of economic value to white South Africans. Nor does it explain how the game eventually changed.

Significant pressure to reform started from the mid-1980s, the same time as economic and sporting sanctions were established. There was also a kind of social embarrassment experienced as South Africa tried to limit freedoms decades after the civil rights movement in the USA and elsewhere. It is possible to evade some of the economic consequences of sanctions but much harder to avoid the stressful stigma attached to them.

Despite pressure from outside, the South African government became more stubborn. To preserve self-identity it followed policy that was self-destructive. This is a common maladaptation, defending the indefensible to maintain a fatally flawed game with actions that are yet more damaging. The aftermath of collapse after stubborn reinforcement can be varying levels of hard or soft, catastrophic or transcendent.

The hardening of positions in South Africa was an attempt at adapting to survive without the imagination necessary to transcend. In place of working together there is a never-ending series of punishments. Oppression caused uprisings which provoked brutality which created support for armed resistance leading to cross-border raids by the army.

At many points the situation appeared to have entered a death spiral where each side thought it would like to cooperate if only the other side felt the same. From the 1980s, the government was led by Pieter Willem Botha who took advice from Samuel Huntington, a political scientist from the USA. Huntington argued that inevitable reforms would encourage violence. To preserve stability the government needed to create a mighty state security system that would use any means necessary. These means included violence, torture, duplicity, deceit, faulty assumptions and purposeful blindness. The use of political science in this way was a barrier to more creative ways of transforming from apartheid. It set in motion a deliberate escalation imposed on emergent political and cultural changes.

By 1985, the ANC aimed to make black townships ungovernable. Its people took over councils and attacked any accused of working for the government. They used petrol bombs, beatings and necklacing – murder caused by burning tyres placed around victims' necks. Debate was stopped using emergency powers, and without legitimate debate came not the hoped-for stability but more extreme resistance.

Their leader, Nelson Mandela, had been in jailed in 1964. He was locked up on Robben Island off the coast of Cape Town. At first, Botha denounced him but then moved him to a prison on the mainland. He was allowed visitors, including foreign reporters. Mandela was offered his freedom, after 21 years, if he would renounce violence. But he refused in a written statement saying that violence was a product of government policy and would not be necessary when full democracy was established.

In 1989, Botha was replaced by FW de Klerk who announced the freeing of Mandela and the unbanning of the ANC just six months after his appointment as president. Despite a very conservative political campaign he chose to lead the *verligte* – enlightened – within his party. He opened negotiations with the ANC to establish a non-racist future.

Within four years, the first free elections were held for all races. De Klerk served as deputy president in a government of national unity for two years and then retired from politics. He was to say later that stability had been restored to South Africa. It was stability made possible by actively making huge changes allowing the country to continue to develop.

It was meant to be a difficult challenge. Teams of hackers and mathematicians entered a computer tournament based on the work of Robert Axelrod, an American political scientist, on cooperation through evolution. Difficult challenges are meant to be complex and so the solutions to the challenge were expected to be long and complicated.

Axelrod set up the tournament for other academics and computer scientists to explore different approaches to how best to cooperate and compete. The tournament and its rules were published in an academic journal inviting contestants to send in their best solutions in the mail.

They were asked to think of the most effective way of solving the prisoner's dilemma if each prisoner gets 200 attempts at deciding whether to defect or stay loyal to their fellow prisoner. The prisoners find out what they have both chosen only after they have decided the first time; they can then decide whether to change their minds or keep playing as before. They may decide to defect always, stay loyal always, move randomly between defection or loyalty or adjust their actions based on those of the other prisoner.

To everyone's surprise, the winning entry was just four lines of code from a professor of psychology, Anatol Rapoport. Each line contained one rule. And those four rules were remarkably effective at encouraging cooperation. They follow a strategy called tit-for-tat where the player will cooperate or punish in direct response to the opponent's previous action.

The past matters; but only the immediate past. It doesn't matter what has happened the move before or the move before that, because the player forgives the past. The only action that matters is the one that has just been completed. As a result, it will always pay the opponent to cooperate, regardless of previous history of punishments.

The first rule: unless provoked the player will always cooperate. The second rule: if provoked the player will retaliate. The third rule: the player is quick to forgive. And the fourth rule: the player has a good chance of competing against the same opponent more than once.

Anatol Rapoport was an anti-war and an active pro-peace campaigner. He created his solution to the computer challenge to demonstrate simple ways in which players could learn to embrace cooperation rather than conflict. His experience in the Second World War led him to dedicate his working life to establishing the legitimacy of peace studies. He aimed to 'kill the institution of war' by showing the benefits of cooperation patterns.

In the transition from prison to presidency, Mandela demonstrated the forgiveness part of this tit-for-tat strategy. By putting the past behind him, he was able to deal with his opponents on the basis of what they did rather than what they had done in the past. De Klerk responded in a similar way when he released Mandela from jail; he worked on the basis of what had just happened, the previous move. He freed up his actions.

Many researchers feel these simple rules of niceness, provocability, transparency and forgiveness may provide clues into how human societies work cooperatively. In healthy societies, people learn quickly to work with someone on the basis of the most recent events. Bad behaviour is punished consistently in a proportionate way before starting afresh.

It is not the punishment that is interesting in the game. It is the way that forgiveness resets the game that is particularly instructive. Without forgiveness the game must continue as a round of punishments, and in the real world those punishments would probably increase over time. To forgive is a rule operating out of step that allows the game to change.

Successful adaptation relies on cooperation just as much as competition; there is generally more to win in cooperating than competing. This is particularly so if competition is destructive since it removes value from the game being played. You win but you lose. The best long-term adaptation is to find a way of working together again regardless of previous actions.

Human culture has this forgiveness built in at some level and in some people. We seem to have evolved the ability to be nice even when it does not serve our short-term benefit. Where it works, inherited cultural memory is able to look in the future by relying on very long-term experience. It tells most people, most of the time, that some give and take are necessary to avoid slipping into bloody, vengeful hell on earth.

Video-game designers delve into game theory and make it practical because they want to model reality in the most interesting ways possible to create fantasy worlds with mechanics that engage video gamers. To avoid just one dominant strategy ruining the game, they spice things up.

One way of spicing things up is to use intransitive moves. A form of game like 'paper, rock, scissors' where there is no single strategy that always wins because everything can be beaten, and can beat, something else. One move is related to another move which in turn is related to the original move. This intransitive set-up forces players into more nuanced moves.

As one game designer describes it: 'Consider a game where one kind of unit has long-range attacks, which is defeated by a short-range attacker who can turn invisible; this in turn is defeated by a medium-range attacker with radar that reveals invisible units; and the medium-range attacker is of course weak against the long-range attacker.'

In 1999, David Meyer, the father of quantum game theory, suggested that games played with quantum rules would be very different from those played with traditional rules. He tells a story based on the science fiction series *Star Trek* featuring Captain Picard, played by suave, bald Patrick Stewart. Our brave captain is visited by Q, an all-powerful alien, who threatens to destroy the starship. It's a thought experiment designed to show quantum strategies.

The only way to save his crew is to avoid losing a game of heads and tails with an electron. The electron will be in either a spin-up or a spin-down state which cannot be seen by the captain. Picard must simply make a series of guesses. The captain decides to choose spin-up and then keep flipping the electron. In this way he will win as often as he loses.

What Picard doesn't know is that the electron can be in both spin-up and spin-down states at the same time – a superposition. They hide the electron in a box in a spin-down position. Q uses his first turn to put the electron into a super-position. Picard makes his completely ineffective move by turning the electron. And then Q makes his move returning the electron to its original state that will always be spin-down.

Using these rules means that Q will win every single game, because the electron is always in two positions at once. This makes Picard's attempt to change the situation ineffective because it still leaves the electron in two positions. And Meyer, described by some as the father of quantum strategies, suggests the potential superiority of a game played with quantum rules which overcome limitations of traditional games.

In a way described by Einstein as 'spooky', quantum mechanics has revealed how particles and even objects can become entangled. Even at long distances objects have already been shown to have an information connection which operates at many thousands of times faster than light.

It appears likely, at a molecular level, that nature has taken advantage of this in playing its games of adaptation and survival. At a higher level, every move in a game communicates information which changes the nature of subsequent moves. Even when nothing is done, there is intention. Even when there is no obvious way in which intention is communicated to other players in system or society, there is an effect.

Quantum games are those in which individual moves are entangled so that they are no longer independent. It becomes impossible for one move to be made without a consequence for other moves. This is true even if that consequence is not a conscious one on the part of another player.

Problem games, like the UBS culture of extravagantly risky expansion, or the Israeli–Palestinian conflict, can be transcended by what appear to be out-of-turn moves. These moves are unexpected, and overcome their lack of movement by provoking cooperative moves from the other sides in the game. And these are most likely when someone has been sensitized enough to the needs and fears of others.

If you want to be radical, then listen to other people. The ability to empathize can develop the adaptation required to change the way that a game is played. Mandela in prison appears to have transcended his circumstances, an ability to use empathy to out-emote his opponent as well as out-think him. When he says the best way to defeat an enemy is to make him your friend, he is explaining how he outwitted the game.

These examples suggest the danger of clinging onto stability at all costs. For UBS, it became almost impossible to accept the need to be smaller and less complex in the short term. Even after admitting toxic debts of more than $50 billion it required a further loss of $2.5 billion due to fraud and the subsequent loss of its CEO for those changes to be seriously considered.

For Israel and Palestine, it has become almost impossible to move beyond the sabotage of extremist groups and logic of one-sided expansion. Even after tens of thousands of killings and a direct cost of more than $1 trillion to the Israelis, they so far are unable to understand the nature of the adaptation needed or be capable of making those adaptations happen.

While for South Africa, a way was found of changing the focal point of the game to allow players from all sides to choose between alternative outcomes. Unexpected behaviour from various people and groups involved altered the flow of the destructive game of apartheid. Stability of actions was sacrificed to shift significant groupings in society to a new place, not perfect but one in which democracy was made possible without war. The danger of stability was avoided by not believing in the illusion of stability.

Rule

6

Stupid survives until smart succeeds

'We were wrong, terribly wrong,' wrote Robert S McNamara 30 years after the Vietnam War ended with the fall of Saigon. 'We were wrong,' said John Doerr, the Michael Jordan of venture capital, admitting his mistake in turning down Twitter. 'We were wrong,' explained Edgar Bronfman, boss of Warner Music, accepting the error of going to war with consumers. 'We were wrong,' claimed Ofra Strauss, chair of one of Israel's largest dairy manufacturers, confessing that competition was causing problems.

It's hard to say you're wrong. The challenge is to realize what's wrong before it's too late to put it right, and before the unintended consequences of a wrong decision become unwelcome and unmanageable. Yet for many, many reasons, we find it difficult as individuals to see our errors once we have committed to a certain course of action. And we can find it even more difficult if we have made the wrong decision with other people who share the same biases and self-interest as we do in not seeing our errors.

In 1958, Pedro Bach-y-Rita suffered a severe stroke and collapsed. Aged 65, he was a professor of Spanish at the City University in New York. The damage to Professor Bach-y-Rita's brain was massive. Disturbance in its blood supply destroyed parts of his brain functionality. After his stroke, he was hardly able to speak or move; his face was paralysed along with half of his body.

Helpless, he was confined to a wheelchair by his doctors. The prognosis was hopeless. His sons, one a doctor, Paul, the other, George – still at medical school – were told that there was nothing that could be done for their father. The damage to his brain could not be repaired and would not heal.

The original plan was for him to rehabilitate at the American British Hospital in Mexico. After four weeks he was still unable to move. The treatment ended at that point because it was not believed that long-term rehabilitation could improve stroke sufferers. George brought him back home and decided that there was still progress to be made.

He decided to teach his father to crawl basing his approach on how babies learn. He explained to his father how they would start from the beginning again. They bought kneepads and they got him to crawl supported by a wall for several months. Then he moved to crawling in the garden which led to disapproval from the neighbours who felt it was undignified.

They would play games, rolling marbles for him to catch, or throwing coins on the floor for him to pick up. Gradually he improved. He learned how to sit down and eat with his son. He moved from crawling to shuffling on his knees. He learned to stand again and walk unaided. After three months of practice his speech began to return. A few more months he started to type.

Within 12 months, the professor was back teaching full-time in his old job at City College. He continued until his retirement at 70 whereupon he got another job in San Francisco and remarried. Seven years later, he climbed a mountain in Colombia, suffered a heart attack at 9,000 feet and died aged 72.

The story is remarkable enough as an example of human adaptability but the results of the autopsy revealed much more. The damage to Pedro's brain was much more extensive than thought. And the lesions had not healed. Ninety-seven per cent of the nerves that connect the spine to the cerebral cortex had been destroyed.

His brain had found a way of adapting. It had reorganized itself to change the function of parts to replace the functionality of damaged parts. The constant work with George had given his brain the prompts to use existing tissue in new ways. Upon making the discovery, Paul returned to medical practice, retrained and dedicated his working life to understanding better how to stimulate the natural adaptability of the brain.

This area of study was not entirely new; the idea first appeared in 1890 from a psychologist named William James but it had been pretty much ignored for 50 years. It waited for a name until the 1950s when neuroscientist Jerzy Knorski coined the term neural plasticity. Until the 1970s the accepted view was that the nervous system, including brain functions, was fixed. The brain could not repair itself nor be repaired. Only the work of scientists like Paul Bach-y-Rita changed the majority view.

He demonstrated that parts of the brain that usually do one thing can be retrained to do something else entirely. In one demonstration, images from a head-mounted video camera are sent to the tongue of a blindfolded volunteer. The camera sends enough visual information to allow people to catch balls rolled towards them. They can't see through their eyes. They can 'see' through their brains and it doesn't matter whether the eye or a camera is sending the information.

Bach-y-Rita proposed a life cycle of plasticity where visible progress in adapting slows while invisible, deep progress adapting the brain's connections continues. The lack of progress tempts therapists and patients to stop rehabilitation efforts at exactly the point that the brain-body needs to be stimulated. People severely damaged by strokes who had previously been written off as beyond help could now be rehabilitated by accessing the brains inbuilt adaptability.

The story is also about the adaptability of science, of human knowledge. It is a demonstration of how science seeks to disprove its own theories in search of more and more useful theory. Over the long term theory adapts to discovery, to evidence. But it can only do so if someone challenges existing limitations. For as long as any constraint is accepted, there can be no new knowledge that goes beyond it.

One of the more famous voices in how science adapts was Thomas Kuhn, a physicist by training, from Cincinnati, who published his best-known work in 1962 while at the University of California, Berkeley. *The Structure of Scientific Revolutions* argued that knowledge does not grow in a consistent way. Paradigms shift from time to time to make new theories and discoveries possible.

It was impossible for treatment of stroke sufferers to get beyond a certain point without a paradigm shift in the way that brains were understood. Neuro-plasticity had to compete with the idea that brain tissue was fixed. Part of the competition is objective, based on evidence. Part is subjective, based on the assumptions that guide how the credibility of new theories is assessed.

The challenge then is to stay open to new paradigm shifts without becoming obsessed with the new, new thing at the expense of progress. The new way of looking at situations isn't necessarily better than the old way. But to avoid new thinking is to reduce the effectiveness of adaptation. Unhelpful, unworkable, illogical, even false ideas can survive simply because people are not ready to listen to a smarter alternative. And it's a lesson that is useful to any kind of adaptive effort: be open to the absurd and insignificant.

In 1995, CEO Robert DiRomualdo had every reason to feel pleased. Under his leadership, bookseller Borders had grown from just 31 stores to more than 350 units, and from $59 million to nearly $1.4 billion in sales. He was the darling of analysts. Even better, the company was on the verge of breaking away from the ownership of giant retailer Kmart. He would be in complete control of his own future. He had never heard of Jeff Bezos. It would be 18 years before that seemed like a huge mistake.

Amazon.com went live in 1995, just five years after the World Wide Web was invented by Tim Berners-Lee. It was part of its founder's 'regret minimization framework' through which he pushed himself to jump into the internet boom of the late 1990s. Back then there were only 16 million web users; today there are over 2 billion. It was hugely exciting to early adopters but to 99.6 per cent of the world it was just another techie thing for computer geeks. This year, Amazon had $45 billion in sales and is only 18 years old.

Back in 1917, Barnes and Noble were also innovators. It was a start-up partnership between William Barnes, son of the owner of a book-printing business, and G Clifford Noble. The first store opened in New York City and specialized in the student book market. They adapted the concept of the cafeteria to create the booketeria, with a conveyor belt with payment taken by one employee, purchases recorded by another and wrapping by a third. They were an early adopter of 'music by musak' playing in the background interrupted by advertising. The flagship store had a staff of more than 300 and became the world's largest bookshop.

Despite this early success, the company was sold in 1971 for $750,000 to Leonard Riggio, a young entrepreneurial bookselling genius from the Bronx. The company was in a slump so Leonard moved beyond textbooks to all non-fiction and beyond students to the general public. He improved the buying experience by creating new more specific categories (a revolution at the time) and introduced a children's section.

These early improvements led to growth. And the success encouraged Riggio to do something bigger. He decided to go for something dramatically different by becoming the first to adapt the supermarket model to bookselling. B&N were the first bookstore in the USA to advertise on television and the first to discount bestsellers in a pile-them-high, sell-them-cheap approach. His book warehouse spanned three buildings and was soon full of customers filling their shopping carts with bargains they might never read.

While Riggio was innovating aggressively at 20 locations, Tom and Louis Borders opened their first store in Michigan. Both students at the University of Michigan, they decided to sell books to the academic community. Over the next few years, they opened four more bookstores, two in Michigan, one in Indianapolis, and another in Atlanta. They had reached $32 million in revenue, and wanted to go much further.

Where Barnes & Noble had Leonard Riggio, the Borders brothers found Robert DiRomualdo. He was a young guy with a Harvard MBA and lots of experience working his way up to become CEO of Hickory Farms, the US food chain. And in 1988, he joined a bookselling industry that was experiencing never-before-seen demand from customers who seemed to have an insatiable demand for discounted books. Borders quadrupled in size over the next four years, and had become a bookselling phenomenon by 1992.

Instead of floating the company on the stock exchange, the brothers decided to sell to the Kmart Corporation. Over the next year, sales reached $224.8 million and the company continued to become more corporate. They gained modern cash registers, a department of human resources, formal training programmes, and a music department. They also developed what many described as the industry's most advanced inventory management system that identified 55 different seasonal patterns.

Within three years, sales of the Borders group were $1.5 billion. They had become a national chain while still keeping, and rewarding, many long-term employees. Most of their people were college graduates and took pride in their ability to deliver the kind of first-class, knowledgeable service customers want and act upon. The Borders concept grew ever larger to the quivering delight of analysts. By 1995, they had 88 superstores; awesome, multi-million-dollar temples for worshippers of literature, music and coffee. The average store stocked more than 128,000 book titles and 57,000 music titles and cost over $2.6 million from decision to opening ceremony.

2006 was the last time the company made a profit. Over the next four years its sales reduced by $1 billion dollars. Eventually it got to the point where each day they were in business they lost money. A succession of chief executives with no bookselling experience attempted various desperate measures without ever getting ahead of the situation. They were never able to understand what was happening and what had to happen well enough to adapt fast enough to survive.

Before the end of 2011, Borders had ceased to exist. It went into bankruptcy protection with $1.2 billion in assets against $1.3 billion in debts and no way to borrow more money. By the end of September, all 19,600 employees had lost their jobs and every store had either been sold or abandoned. Not one of the last four CEOs helped the company to adapt any faster or better.

There was CEO Phillip Pfeffer who lasted five months before resigning in 1999. He was the last bookseller to manage the company. CEO Ron Marshall forced experienced senior managers out and closed down the international divisions, shutting down the benefits of operating in faster-growing economies. He did all that in a year and then quit.

Employees witnessed interim CEO Michael Edwards leading the company near to the bitter end. And finally, venture capitalist CEO Bennet S LeBow, who thought he could buy and sell the company for a profit and failed. None of these men was able to know the problems of the company and the shape of the solution well enough to solve them.

At some point, events will prompt someone in a group, organization or profession to think about adapting to get ahead of future events. It might be anyone at any level or in any role; hierarchy can be inversely related to insights about the future. The further people are from the prodding stimulus of the environment, the less pain they feel. Even if they experience some discomfort, they may find it difficult to know what specific adaptations to make because they can't feel the specific demands of the situation.

People always know. The problems that shock analysts and stock markets are rarely a shock to the rest of the organization. Unfortunately, both insights and dissatisfaction may simmer for years, without reaching boiling point. This is particularly true if they are at a level below internal power and influence, outside the select group who get to make the biggest decisions about the direction of the company.

The problems started years before the crisis. Kmart tried to force Borders to sort out its struggling acquisition, Waldenbooks. As a result, many Borders management resigned. They weren't stupid and couldn't see how they could thrive with the challenges of turning around a problem company. It would slow down their time to adapt.

When Greg Josefowicz became CEO in 1999, the situation didn't look bad financially but the situation was changing at a deep level. He had spent 30 years at a supermarket chain and did not seem to understand how relentlessly the competition was adapting itself and disrupting the market. Even after six years, he didn't solve the integration of purchasing systems between Borders and Waldenbooks. And the lack of integration meant that the company became slower and slower at adapting. Great ideas didn't happen because they were impossible without state-of-the-art computer systems.

In a blunder of epic proportions, the new CEO shut down their newly launched online bookshop after just one year in operation. Yes, it was late. Six years behind Amazon, 12 months behind Barnes & Noble. But shutting it down and replacing it with a co-branded version of the Amazon.com website? The decision handed over the next seven years of learning to their key rival. The technologies, the patents, the recruitment of talent, the knowledge of customer patterns and needs, and the view of the future were all cut off.

Bookselling had never really been about bricks and mortar. It had always been about sharing authors' ideas in ways that customers were willing to pay to enjoy. Barnes & Noble understood. They were slower than Jeff Bezos at recognizing how the web would shape consumer behaviour, but they still took barnesandnoble.com public within two years of amazon.com. That's impressive catch-up adaptation.

As a result of still playing the game of adaptability against amazon.com, they still kept learning from experience and their competition. It's one of those positions where each rival benefits from moves designed to get ahead of a rival. Together, and with others in the industry, including Sony and Apple, they are grow-ing the market. Together with the other players they are moving further ahead of non-players.

So while amazon.com were first to develop an e-book reader – the Kindle – barnesandnoble.com were still able to bring out a viable alternative – the Nook – within a couple of years. Borders took another year to even start selling e-books. The service was provided by a third party. And they never did develop an e-book reader of their own. The difference is significant, more than enough to slow or stop any effective adaptation.

Every situation provides information. If you know what the situation is demanding then you can try to adapt but the connection between situation and response can be damaged. The connection can get slower. It can stop working. Or it can send distorted signals. A disconnect between what the situation needs and what is done can become permanent. You can have a chronic mismatch between situation, intention and action.

In 1969, Bach-y-Rita had a short article published in the journal *Nature*. He described a 400-lb device that allowed people born blind with damaged retinas to see. His machine performed miracles but so absurd were his claims that the story was largely ignored, his papers rejected. In 1994, DiRomualdo appeared unaware of the opportunities in the insignificant world of internet retail, and settled for playing a losing game.

The idea that people would buy their books sat at personal computers and via mobile phone was absurd. Human brains and human society are plastic, they actively try to rewire and reconfigure. What we call competition is only part of this; the bigger picture is that our adaptation to new forms is a deep but imperfect ability.

Part

2

Understand necessary adaptation

Recognizing you need to adapt is a good start, but it's not enough. You may see that there is a problem but that won't necessarily lead to a solution. You may see that there are opportunities but that doesn't mean you will successfully take advantage of them. Without understanding what adaptation is necessary, the wrong actions become more likely.

Moving directly from recognition to action is tempting. The second step is often skipped because of impatience to get on with doing something. We are not all experienced in thinking better together, in finding the root causes of the problems we are facing, or in the art of combining different opinions and insights. Yet to jump straight into action can be a mistake.

We may prefer the comfort of opinions that agree with us, but we need the discomfort of rebels. We may prefer to work alone in glorious isolation, but there is nothing glorious in counterproductive effort. We humans create our own boxes. We may complain about them but not realize that we are part of what we dislike. We are our own constraints.

Moving to a better understanding of what kind of adaptation is required requires a willingness to experiment, but also the collective ability to learn from those experiments. It is easier for most people in a group setting to recognize that something went wrong than to take an honest, blunt, creative look at what has to happen next.

In this section, we will look at the importance of freeing radicals in your group to contribute. It is also important to free the radical natures of some of those in your group so that your good soldiers are able to contribute without feeling disloyal. Truly effective adaptation requires plan B, but also plans X, Y and Z. You can employ imagination to the future and consider possibilities, and you can react with imagination to events.

There's a huge difference between deep and shallow adaptation. It's easy enough to rearrange, restructure or rebrand without changing the deep nature of a social group. Shallow adaptation may look different but feel the same. A shallow change may even work differently but require so much energy that it is only temporary, never really changing the game.

Deep adaptation changes the way a game is played. The situation moves from one state to another, and will remain in more or less the new state until deep adaptation is accomplished again. This is not a static state, it will be dynamic but the game has still changed.

Rule

7

Learning fast better than failing fast

The point of failure is not to fail; the point is to allow failure in the course of learning. To be allowed to experiment and learn from those experiments is valuable. To learn to stop delivering success is potentially disastrous. Just as dangerous is learning to live with varying levels of failure without doing anything to improve the situation.

It can be too easy for individuals and groups to lower expectations. We're not perfect, people start to say. We can't be expected to do it all, they chorus. Well at least we can learn from our mistakes, they reassure each other even after the organization is bankrupt. The point is not to learn *to* fail, but to learn what works *from* failure.

Learning fast involves moving from knowing change is necessary to figuring out what to do differently *and* doing what is necessary. It is the complete movement from insight to action that is relevant to adaptability. You may not notice. You might not react. You may react too little, too late. You may under-react or even overreact.

Overreacting? After PepsiCo rebranded their orange juice brand Tropicana in 2009, sales dropped 20 per cent or $33 million in one month. Competitors benefited as consumers switched brands. The objective had been to reinvigorate the product with a historic marketing and advertising campaign that would 'rejuvenate the category and help consumers'. Within two months of announcing the rebranding Tropicana returned to its original packaging design.

The problem was that the new branding was inoffensive to the point of anonymity. It was criticized for looking like a discount store brand and losing any connection to the tropics. Instead of saying sunshine on the beach, the packaging said buy-one-get-one-free. The criticism came months *before* the launch and it should have been possible to learn from the mistake *before* the mistake cost $33 million.

Even worse, they changed what didn't need changing and left unchanged the juice itself which was facing increasing competition. To be considered premium, orange juice had increased in quality and the discerning buyer was purchasing a clear plastic container without branding. The new packaging did not respond successfully to any of the changes in the competitive situation. Management reverted back quickly but had they learned?

Perfect reacting? The original Mini rolled off the production line in 1959. It was the culmination of a design project prompted by the fuel shortages due to the 1956 crisis in Suez in Egypt. More precisely, it was provoked by the reaction of the CEO of the company who hated the increasingly popular, fuel-efficient German bubble cars and wanted to build a 'proper miniature car'. A small team of eight people designed and built the original prototype – the orange box – led by Sir Alec Issigonis. Mark I of the Mini – originally marketed as the Austin Seven and Morris Mini-Minor – sold more than 1.1 million vehicles while production of all seven versions totalled nearly 5.5 million cars.

The first Mini was not only a proper car; it was also a *proper* adaptation to consumer needs and competitor activities. The company used the failings of its competitors to provide a template for its own design. They successfully adapted existing features that customers would expect through innovation, design and engineering. Then they used their extensive distribution network to get their star adaptation out into the world where it was acknowledged as a design classic. Even the eventual world-famous Mini name came from experimenting. First a dull name following on from other products, then some imaginative play on words, and finally someone *saw the opportunity and grabbed it*. This would be the brand and design that would endure and become world famous.

Under-reacting? Production of the original Mini continued for 41 years. Over that time relatively small changes were made either to save costs or to meet safety regulations. From the 1960s onwards, there was discussion of a modern replacement that would be more practical and refined. Gradually sales fell in export markets despite enduring popularity in its home market.

Internal and external politics delayed a response to increasing and ever-improving competition during the 1970s. In 1979, a prototype was designed by the original team but did not reach production. In 1992, yet another attempt was made to make significant changes to the Mini but the attempt was cancelled by management who felt the investment involved was too high to be profitable.

Perfect reacting? After the BMW takeover in 1994, another project began, this time to design a completely new Mini and benefit from the Mini's fashion icon status around the world. The idea emerged with BMW management who sanctioned first a prototype and a new production car. When the Rover Group was dismantled in 2000, the idea and brand survived in the new ownership of BMW. After a design competition, a decision was made and the first new BMW Mini rolled off the Cowley production line in 2001 with around 2 million produced by 2011.

Rather like the reaction that brought about the first Mini, people at BMW noticed an opportunity to adapt the existing situation. They had realized that BMW needed to increase car sales to stay competitive and that the BMW brand might be damaged if they started production of small cars directly. They saw great potential in existing brands owned by Rover. So they bought Rover and invested in projects that would help develop those brands. And eventually sold everything they didn't want.

BMW were not trying to fail fast. They were trying to learn fast from their acquisition of Rover so that they could achieve their own objectives. Their $2.8 billion investment was not lost since the improvements from the investment went with them. On the BMW side, it was not the failure that some critics have concluded. It was ultimately an impressive demonstration of super-adaptation that has brought in revenues of over £20 billion.

This kind of super-adaptation requires people to try to find ways of transcending the limitations of a particular situation. Those ways may be obvious but generally require creativity mixed with knowledge to discover and put into action. There have to be individual belief and desire to overcome constraints. There have to be opportunities for groups to put their insights to work.

The ideal blend is stubborn, open, obsessive focus on learning by doing. The learning doesn't stop when something goes wrong but neither does the doing. The people in the organization may be curious intellectuals but they want more than knowledge; they want results through knowledge. And that requires a sometimes uncomfortable mix of encouraging people to experiment – which will bring some failures – and also refusing to accept failure as the final, or even general, outcome.

Making the same mistakes for the same reasons is a failure to learn. Even making new mistakes for the same reasons is a failure to learn. The most effective adaptation happens when thought is given to the reasons for failure so that they can be avoided and new lessons learned. Why did it happen last time? What were the assumptions? Did the likely reasons for failure occur before we failed?

Did Tropicana fail because they just tried something risky? Did designers fail because they followed Feng-shui and the Golden Mean rather than understanding how people would feel? Was there testing to find out how people might react? Or was it an unfortunate combination of packaging changes at a time of great uncertainty?

It is ineffective to discourage experimentation. But it is also ineffective to encourage a kind of failure that isn't teaching anything. If someone is paying attention to what they attempt, they can learn from it. They can even try to find out what doesn't work. But if failure is merely the absence of success, then why encourage it at all? And if you're learning too slowly then collapse – some kind of final failure – is a possibility.

There's a balance in adaptability between learning too slow and failing too fast. In 1940, Hitler issued the 'führer directive' that stopped all research and development on projects that would take more than six months to deliver usable weaponry. As a result, he stopped smart minds adapting to the threat of the Allies and handed an advantage to the Allies, who continued to experiment without unhelpfully inflexible deadlines.

People already knew the work was urgent on both sides of the war. The Allies were able to make up lost ground in out-adapting their enemy because they were working under different conditions and systems. Their success supports the idea that adaptability benefits from a particular behaviour and culture. If true, we can learn how to create those conditions.

On 30 October 1939, an idea for a working proximity fuse was proposed by William Butement, a leading member of the team that invented radar. The benefit of a proximity fuse is that it allows a bomb to explode when it is sufficiently close to the target. Without a proximity fuse, bombs relied on timers set on launch or direct contact with something. A bomb could pass within millimetres of the target and still be wasted.

The proposal led to prototypes. The prototypes led to test results and also to a shortage of resources for further development. Yet because of agreement between the USA and UK to share ideas, the project was continued by the US Naval Research Laboratory. Once in production, proximity-fused ammunition was successful in defending against kamikaze attacks in the pacific and neutralizing V-1 bomb attacks in the UK.

After demands from General Eisenhower, proximity fuses were also used in the Battle of the Bulge in 1944. This major German offensive caught the Allies by surprise at a poorly defended part of their lines during heavy cloud cover that grounded air defences. The proximity fuse was used to hugely increase the effectiveness of US artillery and overcome the initial advantages of the surprise attack. It even inspired a minor mutiny among German soldiers who had expected to hide successfully from distant gunners.

Adaptation is a game within a game within a game. There are rules to be discovered. There are rules to be changed or broken or ignored. And there are turns to be taken. Each action contributes to other games in an infinite, and occasionally vicious, regress. Winning positions may be lost by your bad move or by a move by any other player.

Apple does not like to fail in public. If it's going to do something it will do that something as beautifully and completely as possible. Under Steve Jobs's leadership, Apple attempted to learn fast in a number of ways.

First, when it does fail it seeks to rapidly recognize and respond to the problem, including pulling the product from sale, dropping the price, or making immediate improvements. If public reception to a product is negative, Apple notices and acts.

In 2008, when an online service called MobileMe received mainly critical reviews, the CEO summoned the team responsible to a meeting. He asked them what the product was 'supposed to do'. Someone answered and Jobs reportedly shot back, 'Then why the f*** doesn't it do that?'

Jobs then sent an email to employees accepting the product was 'not up to Apple's standards'. Apple offered free extensions to subscribers and announced a replacement service called iCloud. When asked whether it would 'just work' he said 'Why should I believe them? They're the ones that brought me MobileMe!'

Second, when it does fail, it goes back and takes a very hard look at the problems and relentlessly reworks until it becomes successful. Learning from Newton, the failed hand-held computer surfaced in the iPod, iPhone and iPad. Learning from failed videogame console Pippin and failed Macintosh TV became useful for the wildly successful iTunes and Apple TV. And it learned all about beautiful industrial design even after the Apple Cube (an 8 × 8 × 8 translucent cube) failed to sell.

Third, it has shifted some of the experimentation to its partners who have produced the half a million apps and hundreds of peripherals that improve the product offering without damaging the brand. Every app, every peripheral, succeed or fail, can provide fast learning. Some of the best features have been fed back into new versions of Apple's iOS operating system or even into new products like their Amazon competitor – iBooks.

Hating to fail in public doesn't have to be about avoiding learning. Instead of playing safe, you can just play to win. You can refuse to waste valuable lessons by not trying again. Many organizations try things with disappointing results and stop. They may even try yet more things that fail and stop again. Others try things with disappointing results and refuse to change. But the smartest, most adaptive organizations identify something worth doing and keep on learning until they get it right. Even if it takes decades.

Rule
8
Plan B matters most

The Rooney Rule is beautiful. It is perfectly adapted to its purpose. Back in 2002, there were just two black head coaches from 32 teams in the whole National Football League. This was despite more than 70 per cent of the players in the NFL being black.

If the league wanted to change the situation, it would have been impossible to insist that a certain percentage of head coaches were black because specific teams would have been forced to choose black candidates. It would not have been fair because it would have only applied to a certain number of teams, not to everyone.

If the league wanted to change the situation only through passively encouraging a change in perceptions with poster campaigns and training programmes, it might have never happened because of the deep equilibrium that was keeping things as they were. White owners know white players who come to mind when a vacancy arises. Owners don't have to be consciously racist to not appoint players they don't think of or don't know. There was a cultural and processual reason for high numbers of white coaches.

There were too few black candidates getting interviews to change perceptions. If you never interview, or rarely interview, a candidate from outside your own experience you're unlikely to hire one. Even if qualified. If candidates aren't being interviewed then they are less likely to apply for the positions. It is a self-perpetuating cycle. Self-perpetuating cycles require intervention, some kind of breakthrough change of the pattern so it is allowed to gradually lose its negative impact. They need a plan B.

The beauty of the Rooney Rule is that it only insists that black candidates are interviewed. The owner gets to hire whoever he, or she, wants. The rule only ensures that the club has to think about non-white candidates. The rule disturbs the deep equilibrium that kept things the way there were. It introduces a simple, redesigned part of the process which, in turn, alters perceptions and increases opportunities.

By 2011, the number of non-white coaches had risen to eight. That's still only 25 per cent of the coaching position but there are 400 per cent more coaches than before the rule change. Just as importantly, there has been a year-on-year increase in the number of minority and female executives. The recognition that there is a problem has been matched with action to adapt the situation in a way that minimized friction and maximized progress.

Adaptability doesn't always kick in automatically; it must often be prompted. It's easy enough for adaptation to be screwed up if the need to adapt is not recognized, if the nature of the adaptation is not understood, or if the action to adapt is not taken. At any of these points, effective adaptation is stopped.

It follows that organizations need to find ways of increasing recognition of need to adapt, understanding of action needed, and the action that is required. The design of these interventions should be as elegantly simple as possible, because if the intervention is too complicated it will slow down the adaptability it seeks to speed up. The treatment may be just as damaging as the disease it attempts to cure.

Sometimes there are unintended consequences from well-meaning changes. Changes to stop one problem may increase those problems in the future. This can happen when problems that flow from a deep flaw in the system are repaired superficially. They give the impression of being fixed. They may fool many into believing that all is well; while under the surface problems continue to develop. The consequences of the problem and the cause of the problem get worse because no new attempts are made to adapt the system. Thinking anything is fixed for ever prevents early recognition of new problems.

Equally, a change may make the situation worse because it qualifies as a maladaptation. It is change that is worse suited to the demands of the environment or events than the previous version of the human system. These changes do not merely hide the problem, letting it get worse, hidden in the background; these changes either magnify the original problem or add new problems. They may also represent a worsening of ability to recognize, understand or act in effective ways that adapt to the events or environment.

The Easter Islanders cut down all the trees. They became the poster children of self-inflicted environmental destruction: a reminder that if they could destroy the basis of their prosperity, so could any civilization. A society descended from 40 Polynesian forebears capable of navigating the oceans. A community with the technology to build at least 887 massive stone statues including one unfinished example nearly 70 feet high with a weight of 270 tons. They had independently developed their own form of writing, rongorongo, one of only four independent inventions of written communication in history. They depended on hunting birds in the palm tree forest. How could they have destroyed the forest?

Competing explanations exist for the disappearance of the rainforest. Scientists tend to agree that the deforestation happened over a period of 200 years but there are major differences of opinion over when this happened. They are agreed that around eight major bird species became extinct as a result. It is generally accepted that the islanders had a food economy based on hunter-gathering in the forest and through fishing.

Differences appear over the lessons to be learned. For most, it is a haunting story of extreme maladaptation, with the islanders causing their own problems. For some, it is a heroic story of resourceful adaptation, with the islanders adapting successfully even faced with major environmental challenges. The truth seems to be a mixture of both.

The story of the Rapa Nui begins with the great Polynesian Pacific Ocean exploration force around AD 700. The consensus based on DNA evidence is that groups from Polynesia to the west started to send out exploration groups to find new lands to colonize. Some succeeded, while others failed and abandoned their islands after two or three hundred years. The group of between 30 and 100 people who arrived on Easter Island arrived about AD 700 based on carbon dating of artefacts found there.

It's an isolated place. The nearest inhabited land is Pitcairn Island, some 1,200 miles towards Australia. The closest mainland is the coast of Chile, 2,300 miles away, or Tahiti, another 2,500 miles southeast. Once you're there, your options become limited. Finding raw materials, foraging for food or exchanging new ideas with other groups is difficult.

The group of men, women and possibly children benefited from abundant bird life but were perhaps unaware of the fragility of their rainforest. Jared Diamond points out the island qualified in eight of nine characteristics that make the death of a forest more likely. Its latitude is high, plant-feeding rainfall and soil-enriching dustfall from Asia are both low, it's relatively cold and is the second most isolated island. His statistical modelling suggests that Easter, Nihoa and Necker would be the most deforested, and that's what happened.

In their two giant canoes, the Easter Islanders landed on one of the most fragile environments in the Pacific islands. They were not to know that the domestic rats they brought with them would eat and destroy the roots of the palm trees. They cut down trees for wood and to clear land for crops, not realizing that they would struggle to grow back. Yet they still cut when they should have resisted the urge.

Increasingly elaborate rituals used wood to transport the huge statues and the environment could not support the level of resources needed by their unlimited ambition. They produced more statues than they ever had wood enough to transport. No one was able to acknowledge the need to adapt and understand what was necessary to do so. They could have slowed down production of statues, but in a competitive environment such considerations were ignored. The invisible hand cut down every tree.

Some kind of irrational exuberance, an obsession with grand gestures, led them to carve the sculptures – moai – in the likeness of their god-like chiefs. With their eyes turned to the sky and their backs to the sea protecting the people, they diverted time and resources from more important areas of adaptation. It didn't happen on other islands colonized by Polynesians. Later, the statues appear to have been regretted by the Easter Islanders who knocked over every single sculpture in a display of frustration.

Shortage of food, and the realization of the consequences of their failure to adapt, contributed to internal conflict. This included the making of weapons, and violence between different groups. It isn't clear to what extent they fought before the deforestation but the population dwindled from around 15,000 to fewer than 3,000 in about a century. Twenty-one species of trees and all species of land birds were extinct.

As a result of fighting over resources and loss of population, the Easter Islanders went through a process of adaptation which was painful but did not lead to extinction. They appear to have avoided final failure for their society by deliberately adapting. They turned to farming for food production and may have fertilized their soil because by the time the Dutch arrived in 1722, the soil was rich and under cultivation.

It isn't clear whether the bird cult which developed on the island was a contributing factor to the problem, since it handed the winner of a swimming and climbing race control over resource distribution. Or was it the way the society adapted by moving away from a strict hierarchy based on a divine right of kings, to one based on shared power through a form of meritocracy? It was a campaign race for island leadership.

Hostility towards European ships slowed down the colonization of the island. The Dutch visited for a week in 1722. The Spanish visited in 1770 taking symbolic possession on behalf of King Charles III by erecting three wooden crosses. The island was left pretty much alone until 1862 when slave traders from Peru captured around 1,500 of its people including the son of the chief. They were forced to return their slaves a year later but most of them had already died. The remainder were dumped back on the island with some carrying smallpox which reduced the population further.

The population converted to Christianity in 1866 but the first missionary brought with him tuberculosis which killed another 400 people. Then a French mariner named Jean-Baptise Dutrou-Bonier arrived. He married a local girl by force and appointed her queen and recruited a faction of the islanders who kept him in violent power for four years. He bought almost all of the land but most people left for Tahiti and Mangareva. By the time he was murdered in 1876 for kidnapping children, there were just 111 people left.

The island became an annex of Chile in 1888 with an agreement signed with survivors who lived in one small area while the rest was rented as a sheep farm until 1953. And finally in 1966, the islanders became full citizens of Chile with full protection of their rights. Since then, they have embraced what could be reconstructed of their ancient culture but have continued the struggle to adapt successfully to the twenty-first century.

When I first heard of the Easter Islanders, it was from the crazy expedition of the not-so-crazy adventurer Thor Heyerdahl who had decided to prove that they could have travelled from South America. In his book, *The Kon Tiki Expedition*, he proves settlers could have also travelled from South America. This would explain the existence of the sweet potato and accounts of different skin colours on the island. He built a huge *pae-pae* raft out of balsa wood, a technology of the era in question, and sailed across the Pacific Ocean for 101 days and 4,300 miles. And before that he used imagination to create his theory and go beyond what we had known.

Thinking beyond what we know is a key benefit of imagination. It allows us to anticipate what cannot be seen and understand what has not yet been discovered. Through applying imagination we are able to question assumptions, and through questioning assumptions we are able to extend what is known.

The basis of critical thinking performs thought experiments to explore the extent to which something may be true or false, and to combine existing knowledge in new, boundary-spanning ways. Imagination is used even by those who think they are un-imaginative. Without it they could not perceive anything before it happened and be unable to anticipate well enough to do anything. Those particularly imaginatively able can more powerfully see a more complex set of connections, facts and possibilities.

Path dependency is not deterministic. There is room to move outside the most obvious direction of a path. Even a path that is well worn can be evaded. That's something heartening to those feeling trapped by the limitations of the assumed shape of the future. It can be liberating to see possibilities outside historical precedent. It's also a characteristic that can be unexpected, puzzling and unsettling for those who assumed the safety of the path. To see the sparkling future and see it dimmed. This is loss.

Successful adaptation depends not so much on what has happened before but on what can be imagined next. The events of the past provide the present situation yet the present situation is susceptible to the transformation power of perception. Past, present and future are real yet malleable, which leaves us able to transcend those constraints that depend on our lack of knowledge for their power.

Netflix is a story of disruptive innovation. They are a living, breathing corporate example of how to adapt ahead of assumed behaviours and then how to crash and burn in the horrific detail of the high-definition, super-slow-motion spotlight of public scrutiny. The end of the story may never come, but the story so far is instructive. The comparison between their superlative success in strategic adaptation, figuring out the weakness of their competition, and the dangers of a proposed, pre-emptive adaptation is dramatic.

It all started innocently enough. Netflix saw the future and it was video streaming. The day of DVDs rushed to your door for a subscription fee was the past and it was over. Unfortunately for Netflix, their customers stubbornly refused to see things their way. They kept on signing up for the subscription fees that included DVD delivery. They foolishly believed that they preferred both services, and kept paying for them.

Netflix management, eager to re-educate their customers, decided to stop offering a service that included both DVDs and movie streaming. Instead of being charged $9.99 for unlimited streaming and DVD subscription, customers would have to pay $7.99 for each service separately. The changes were made overnight, with no warning. There were no other options made available; customers could either pay more or go elsewhere. And, given the choice, over one million customers cancelled their subscriptions.

Losing one million customers was bad for Netflix. One million customers represent about 4 per cent of their total. Four in every hundred quit the business, and many of those that remained weren't happy either. Worse, many of the customers who had left were part of the streaming-only group who were annoyed at how the company had acted. The CEO's reaction was to announce they would split the company into two; one for DVDs, the other for online streaming. Stock holders reacted with a 25 per cent fall in share value in just a few hours.

When the Netflix CEO says, 'companies rarely die from moving too fast, and they frequently die from moving too slowly', he confuses moving fast with adapting successfully. Speed is not always a virtue. There is no ideal speed of adaptation because adaptation is linked to the match between environment and actions. You can rush changes through impatience rather than urgency, arrogance rather than ignorance.

It is more accurate to say that companies rarely fail from making the right moves, and they frequently die from making the wrong moves. It is a question of timing rather than of speed, a matter of knows-when rather than know-how. It's possible to adapt slowly and thrive, or make fast changes that are maladaptive or simply superficial.

Back in 1999, Reed Hastings helped change the world of DVD rentals. He launched the company 18 months before as a fairly standard pay-per-rental approach that just happened to have an online store, not a bricks-and-mortar outlet. The idea was to compete with Blockbuster by not having to have traditional overheads.

Things changed when Hastings remembered the irritation of being charged late fees as a customer. His memory prompted the team to adapt their offering. Their flat subscription, unlimited rentals without late fines or shipping fees was an offer that 22 million customers could not refuse. It was also an offer that confused the competition, particularly Blockbuster who spent the next decade trying, and failing, to catch up.

Rewinding back to 1985, it was Blockbuster who had most effectively adapted to the growing demand for movie rentals. Started up in Dallas, Texas by David Cook who applied his expertise in managing large computerized databases to the problem of how best to provide huge choice to customers. He invested $6 million into a warehouse and delivery system that could provide customized stock to individual stores.

Blockbuster caught the attention of Wayne Huizenga who bought the company in 1987 with the intention of expanding as fast and as large as possible. At one point they were opening one store every 17 hours. Alongside which they aggressively expanded through buying other movie rental stores. They sold the business to Viacom for an eye-watering $8.4 billion in 1998 but the market was already changing faster and by 2004 they split from their parent company.

Netflix had helped change the market in a way Blockbuster did not understand well enough to respond with effective adaptation. It should have been easy. They should have been able to simply start up a competing service running a little behind

Netflix. They already had customers. They already had money. They already had brand recognition. But unfortunately they also had something to protect and ingrained ideas about how to best run a movie rental business. They did nothing.

It took them until 2004 to launch their online DVD rental service and another year to drop late fees to match Netflix. In 2007, the next CEO stopped work on the online service and concentrated on the in-store experience because of concerns over profitability but also because he understood retail, not the world of web innovation. He didn't understand the nature of the adaptation required and so decided not to attempt to understand. This was a mistake.

Within three years, the company was delisted from the New York Stock Exchange, and unable to pay interest on over $40 million of bonds. Before the end of 2010, it filed for bankruptcy protection with $900 million in debt. In the time provided by Chapter 11 legislation they had intended to adapt sufficiently to keep all 3,300 stores open. However, in the end they did not have enough cash. The once proud Blockbuster was sold in an auction for $320 million to Dish Network, the country's second largest pay TV operator, who kept about 600 stores open. Six hundred where once there were four thousand.

We are talking about movie rentals but the ideas apply to any deliberate adaptation. It is necessary to recognize the need to adapt, understand the specific adaptation required, and then adapt. It's strange to think a company founded on the basis of a technological shift in movie watching, from cinemas to home videocassettes, could have missed the next big change. This is a reminder that experience does not necessarily lead to insight, understanding or action.

Netflix may triumph, as may Blockbuster. Netflix has over two-thirds of the digital movie market in the USA. Their nearest competitor, Comcast, has 8 per cent and three rivals, DirecTV, Times Warner and Apple, with 4 per cent of the market. Yet it's entirely possible to go too fast for your own good, so far ahead of a trend that it impresses you rather than buyers of the product or service. Or, more precisely, to go fast, go arrogant and fail to take your supporters with you. In matters of adaptability, it is always the beginning.

The problem is that if customers know that a deal is bad for them, it is usually also bad for the company. It isn't planned that way. Netflix thought they could have all the benefits of the changes: increased revenue and a gradual running down of the less-profitable service. Moving from two separate services to two separate companies is intended to safeguard the Netflix brand while eventually quitting the Qwickster market. But if customers know this is bad for them, they will quit and then it is bad for both.

Customers can quite easily survive without Netflix. They can buy DVDs or use other services to rent them. They can go back to Blockbuster who immediately ran a campaign highlighting how 'Netflix raised prices by 60%'. Many of the 22 million Netflix customers have now been prompted to discover the world of free and paid, legal and illegal, movie streaming. They would not have gone looking for alternatives, but now they will.

Small adaptations, like the Rooney Rule, can have powerful beneficial consequences. Obsession with the superficial, like the immense statues of the Easter Islanders, can dramatically reduce opportunities to thrive. This can place great strain on a group's ability to adapt. The Rapa Nui survived but have not, so far, regained their former glories. It is the combination of recognition, understanding and action that permits adaptation.

Rule
9
Free radicals

On the last week of August 2005, the president of Facebook was arrested for felony possession of cocaine. This arrest was used as an excuse to push him out of the company by investors concerned about his influence with founder Zuckerberg. On the afternoon of 22 September 2011, the same Sean Parker will stand alongside the same Mark Zuckerberg to announce changes that may transform the music industry.

The radical returned triumphant although, in truth, he had never really left. He was one of the key reasons for the relentless, restless adaptation that has characterized Facebook. Sean Parker never settles for safe. He never accepts traditional obvious. He distrusted the judgement of early investors. He poked and prodded to keep the company independent. And he outlasted the venture capitalists that pushed him out.

There is a conflict between the forces of chaos and order in human life, but it is not always as the battle is portrayed. In the life of organizations, it is about preference as much as it is about professionalism. There is nothing innately superior about the effectiveness of a tidy desk compared to a messy desk, or to the efficiency of getting you to a better place compared to curiosity-fuelled discovery.

In the life of human groups, the concept of realism can be used as a strategy of political control rather than as an objectively better way of adapting for a better future. It can also be as much about a struggle between people who find uncertainty uncomfortable and those who find certainty unrewarding.

Fear mongering about disorganization can lead to excessive levels of organization that scare away the creative, rebellious behaviour necessary to joyous renewal. If there are sufficient resources, it will work for a time. Until the next technology trend, climate change or social wave exposes traditional approaches as unplanned obsolescence.

Innovators bet on ideas, while entrepreneurs bet on choices. Managers tend to play it safe with predictable promotions, while senior leaders can be tempted by the safety of size either of their organization or their pension pot. They depend on what appears safe. They wish to take advantage of what they can see if life continues as expected. Entrepreneurs and innovators seek the satisfaction of seeing their actions change and shape the future in new ways. They are effectual thinkers.

When times are easy, almost anyone can look effective. The game may become one of the superficial effectiveness which the truly effective cannot win. When choices seem obvious, un-imaginative leaders may be rewarded for making the obvious choices even when they know they're the wrong choices. And if they are able to move on, retire, or die before the consequences of those decisions are known, then bad choices worked.

In 2007, Starbucks was in trouble. It was in so much trouble that the chairman and founder, Howard Schultz, wrote to the CEO, Jim Donald, to warn that the in-store experience was being watered down with a hugely damaging impact on the success of the overall business. It was in so much trouble that the founder of the company came back to be chief executive again. Starbucks was in so much trouble that it had to close 977 stores and lay off 1,000 people in the USA. Customer numbers had reduced for the first time since going public. With profits falling, the share price fell by more than 50 per cent, as investor fear spread about the market in general and Starbucks in particular.

Jim Donald, the new CEO of Starbucks, was handpicked by his predecessor, and this was part of the problem. Instead of adapting to circumstances, the new CEO unthinkingly accelerated actions. There was little room in his decision-making process for nuance. He saw an unbroken pattern of opening new stores and so opened even more. He had spent his time prior to becoming CEO opening stores in the USA so he opened almost all his new stores within the 51 states. There were 900 more stores planned in the USA the year he was forced out of the company. The year Schultz closed 977 stores.

On the day that Jim Donald was appointed, he said nothing about the Starbucks experience. Not one thing. He spoke of being honoured to succeed Orin. He spoke about his optimism for the opportunities ahead. He said the opportunities were virtually endless. He said how proud he was to be part of the world-class management team. But not one word about the people he would be working with or their contribution to the world. Not one word about the world outside the USA. Nothing was said about doing anything incredible or worthwhile or different. He could not have been more inward.

Superficial actions may look almost identical to deep decisions but they are not. They lack the understanding, the intelligence that led to the decision. Actions are relative to circumstance. Opening a store isn't right or wrong. It depends. Increasing efficiency for customers isn't right or wrong. It depends how it is done and when. The problem for the non-radical is that they are driven by everything but the thing itself. Jim Donald wanted to be seen to be successful, and deliver record financial performance. Schultz wanted to create a third place, an authentic, coffee-loving experience.

Orin had a deeper understanding of the mind of his radical mentor. As he made decisions, his mind had learned habits and considerations that kept closer to the ideal. To hear him speak about Starbucks is to hear him in conversation with Schultz. If he mentions efficiency, the voice of Schultz prompts him to underline authenticity. Jim Donald had no Schultz voice in his head warning him to make room for beauty and risk. Instead he had a Smith voice speaking about efficiencies of scale and investment ratios.

When the slowdown really kicked in, Schultz found his own voice again. He saw that the romance and theatre had been lost. He wrote a famous memo that was leaked to the media, chronicling the series of decisions made over the past decade that had stripped the company of the soul of the past. He was stung by criticisms that stores were sterile, cookie cutter, and devoid of passion. This was about far more than making money.

On the afternoon of 26 February 2008, Starbucks closed all 7,100 stores in the USA. A sign on the window of each one read: 'GREAT ESPRESSO REQUIRES PRACTICE. THAT'S WHY WE'RE DEDICATING OURSELVES TO HONING OUR CRAFT.' All 135,000 baristas were retrained on pouring the perfect shot of coffee. They were taught to grind coffee again, instead of relying on automated machines and pre-ground, vacuum packs. In response to a taste test that found McDonald's coffee was better, they experimented with a new roasting process to create a signature blend. Schultz didn't have to weigh profit margin and key management ratios; he just had to deliver what customers loved.

By 2010, Starbucks had recovered. Record revenue of $10.7 billion reflected in stock price increases from $8 to $30. With the radical brain back at the top, so were they.

Radicals can influence the rest of the group under certain circumstances. This influence takes different forms. There are charming radicals who utilize charisma to take people with them. There are also prove-the-world-wrong radicals who attempt the unconventional, absurd or even dangerous so that they can provide evidence that they are right about something that matters to them, intellectually or otherwise.

This influence matters to the adaptability of the group. It's part of the adaptation mechanism because it allows unconventional views about each step. The group is in most danger when circumstances change beyond its recent experience. People don't know what to do that will be successful. They may even be unaware of the need to adapt. Radicals help by insisting upon alternatives and obsessively proving they work.

Robert Lanza altered the genetic code of chickens in his parent's basement when he was 14 years old. Not only was his age remarkable, he was transferring genes from black chickens to white chickens only three years after the genetic code had been deciphered. This was 1969, and while the rest of the country was obsessing about the first lunar landing and kids his age were running around with toy ray guns, he was playing God.

Proud of his achievements, Lanza turned up on the steps of Harvard Medical School with his chickens, or at least the results of his experiments. Professors at the university started to mentor our radical teen and his experiment with the chickens was eventually published in *Nature*, the world's pre-eminent scientific journal.

Robert's childhood was no Bill Gates III story of privilege and opportunity. His family background, from Roxbury, a tough area of Boston, meant that teachers labelled him as slow. They put him in the bottom of the three ability groups in school. Each school day he spent with kids who were failing. Each day after school he roamed the nearby wilderness, rarely allowed to stay inside except to eat and sleep.

He remembers being fascinated by the world. He wanted to understand how his universe worked. His neighbours nurtured him somewhat. If he brought them an insect, they would buy a magnifying glass. If he discovered a bird's egg, they would get a book on ornithology. He was nurtured by neighbours who lent him their perspective on doing the right thing and fighting for the right thing. This viewpoint became part of him.

By the time he was 10 years old, his fifth-grade teacher realized he might have talent and got him to enter the science fair. He came second and realized he didn't have to be restricted by his environment. By eighth grade, his neighbour was his science teacher. She jumped the queue and put him in the high school honours biology class. To prove the doubters wrong, he altered the genetic code of those chickens. He got a C grade.

For two years after graduating from medical school, he did nothing apart from think about how the universe worked. Fresh from his self-imposed sabbatical, he launched into overcoming problems of rejection and tissue shortages in transplanting insulin-producing cells to people with diabetes. His experiments showed that if you surround an organ with the patient's own cells, there is no rejection. He figured it out by injecting islet cells from a patient's pancreas into his portal vein after which they lived happily in the man's liver.

In 1990, he started working for Bill Chick who was dying of diabetes. Bill wanted Robert to save him by making his methods work for insulin. They managed to succeed in making dogs insulin independent. Hearing about Dolly the Sheep, the first cloned mammal accomplished by the Roslin Institute in Scotland, he became certain that using cloned stem cells *from* the sick patient was the answer. Chick wasn't convinced and died.

Undeterred, Lanza joined a cloning company called Advanced Cell Technologies (ACT). Before his work could begin he had to convince the National Institutes of Health to allow cloning of embryos, despite the US public being against such work. He received death threats and the condemnation of the Pope but he also received 50 letters from Nobel laureates and permission to begin his work. Radicals don't stop, which is the source of progress.

As a result of his work, clinical trials began in California and London in 2011 based on embryonic stem cells. It is a trial aimed at regenerating retinal cells from people suffering from macular dystrophy. The condition causes the gradual degeneration of central sight so that sufferers are left with only peripheral vision. This particular, hour-long procedure will inject a suspension of 50,000 cells into the retina of young patients. They have a genetic disorder, Stargardst, which destroys retinal tissue, causing blindness.

Hundreds of scientists are developing treatments with human embryonic stem cells, despite legal restrictions and religious objections. Many of them are led by people who simply will not accept the constraints of tradition or the limits of knowledge. They dream of a day when stem cells will be used to replace all defective body parts. They want to understand how far we can adapt our methods of discovery and how far we can adapt our bodies to overcome genetic flaws.

Intellectual flexibility is more important than intelligence quotient when solving what has not been solved before. The obsessive desire to understand and improve shown by Sean Parker, Howard Schultz and Robert Lanza drag thinking and action forward. They can't help themselves, they radicalize whatever they touch. They get bored by the same-old-same-old even when it's lucrative. They kick against the pricks of the status quo. They disturb old alliances and poke at wasps' nests of convention.

Back in 1966, when Robert Lanza was still struggling in fifth grade, Professor Liam Hudson of Cambridge was identifying two types of clever schoolboy. He was interested in the creative theories of Getzels and Jackson who proposed in 1960 that a high IQ is not clear indication of high ability. He administered the Getzels–Jackson tests to 95 students and found that they were of two types: convergents and divergents.

Convergents look for one answer to any problem. They rapidly sorted through any wrong answers to determine which one was correct. If they already knew an answer they would use it without consideration or delay. They jumped into the task with enthusiasm, interested in finding the predetermined answers to predetermined questions.

Divergents create as many answers to a problem as possible. The game is to generate options and possibilities. They see little interest in repeating what is already known. They cannot easily accept the limitations of a one-answer approach to knowledge or life. As a result they find IQ tests boring, do badly at them. They don't value tests, so many of the people who overvalue tests undervalue them. Yet these are our radicals, those who can see new possibilities. And in times of great uncertainty or new challenge, we need them.

Hudson found that 75 per cent of those who were convergents excelled at the physical sciences while 75 per cent of those who were divergents excelled at the arts and social sciences. More of those gifted at creating additional options choose to follow subjects that respect nuance and complexity beyond the one right way. This has significant consequences for adaptability where small and large groups require diverse alternatives to better match effective action to uncertain situations.

Adaptation benefits from a healthy mix of convergent and divergent approaches. Once a solution is found that pretty much works, it requires stability for it to work over and over again. Those who inherit knowledge are able to use it until those who create knowledge replace their legacy. The knowledge creators, the radicals and the rebels permit adaptation.

Rule
10
Think better together

Lysistrata is a comic play first performed in 411 BC in ancient Athens. Written by Aristophanes, it tells the story of the efforts of one woman to bring an end to a war being fought between Athens and Sparta. She convinces women throughout Greece to withhold sex from all men for as long as the fight continues.

In the play, men from both sides become desperate for sex and agree to peace talks. Lysistrata introduces them to a beautiful young woman named Reconciliation. The thought of her, symbolic of all that is good about peace, encourages delegations to settle their arguments. There is peace at last, and rowdy celebrations begin in the Acropolis.

The main character in the play is fictitious, although the war was real without an easy or rapid end. It lasted for 25 years during which an ending probably seemed impossible. After the play was first performed, another seven years of war followed, ending in the partial end of democracy and reduction in Athenian prominence.

In September 2006, a group of wives and girlfriends of gangsters in the town of Pereira, Colombia announced a sex-strike to encourage the ending of violence. Called the 'strike of crossed legs' it succeeded in sending the message that killing was not sexually attractive and resulted in a 26.5 per cent decline in murders. In April 2009 a group of Kenyan women organized a week-long sex-strike; they encouraged the wives of politicians to support them and even offered to pay prostitutes for lost earnings.

But by far the most dramatic of the sex-strikes was in Liberia where Leymah Gbowee organized a series of mass non-violent protests. The non-obvious adaptation of Liberian women to their 14-year civil war succeeded in establishing peace. By 2005, their campaign also helped elect their new president, Ellen Johnson Sirleaf, the first female president on the African continent. Both women received the Nobel Peace Prize.

By 2002 more than a quarter of a million people had been killed in Liberia. That's the year Leymah Gbowee decided that changes would have to come from the mothers. She had spent years working with ex-child soldiers as a trauma counsellor and social worker. It was this experience that helped her find a non-obvious answer to protests against the war.

It would be the women who changed the rules of the game. The women who started singing together in a fish market in the capital. Women were unhappy with their children dying in the conflict. Women pressured Charles Taylor, dictator, to start peace talks. Women marched into the hotel where negotiations had stalled. And it was women who dared the negotiators to sign a comprehensive peace treaty with a new government.

The significance of the Liberian story is that the dictator was out-thought and out-adapted by the women's movement. They brought Christians and Muslims together, something the government couldn't do. Through non-violence, including the sex-strike, they made their voices heard. They recognized that adaptation was necessary, understood what that needed to be, and were better organized than the various warring factions.

Most of the time, successful adaptation is about thinking better. This may include hard work but that's rarely the primary difference between one way and a better way. Intelligence is the ability to adapt to situations, or wherever possible, it is the ability to adapt situations to our requirements. It is the ability to see patterns of behaviour and creatively respond to them so that those patterns change in some way that is desired.

After the civil war ended, with the leader of the dictatorship on trial on war crimes charges, Gbowee led calls for a process of truth and reconciliation in a similar way to the successful adaptations in South Africa and Northern Island. It was also an echo of *Lysistrata*, where reconciliation is a beautiful woman who signifies all that peace can bring.

Human adaptation can be genetic, technological or behavioural but attempts to adapt culture or social behaviour require collective support to be successful. This collective does not need to start with majority support; it often starts with an individual who finds a small core of supporters who then improve the arguments and methods necessary to move a majority to action.

One person who investigated the process of convincing a majority to alter collective behaviour is Peter Hedström, one of the founders of analytical sociology. Hedström, Professor of Sociology at Oxford, focuses his research on complex social networks. He wants to understand how social mechanisms work well enough to describe them in detailed, precise ways.

Modern computing has allowed social scientists to start analysing complex human interactions. Some of this work attempts to model human behaviour based on researcher assumptions. Other work examines known human interactions to discover patterns that reveal social mechanisms.

Hedström created computer models that looked at what is necessary for a large social group, a corporation, or even a society, to change direction. He criticizes simple economic models because they assume everyone makes decisions in a rational way with perfect information about the best available choices.

Hedström's models suggest that the majority does not need to be convinced for them or an organization to take actions in a particular direction. There need only be a majority at the highest level to convince a majority in most groups. Imagine one hundred people in an organization divided into 10 groups of 10 people.

If six in the top team decide on an action, the other four will probably follow. If the top team convinces six people, in five other groups, then each of those groups will probably follow. The likely result is that the rest of the organization will follow the lead of those six groups. This seeming majority is achieved with only 36 people in agreement.

Even fewer people are needed in a very hierarchical organization, such as a traditional corporation. This can be very useful in making rapid decisions where the hierarchy is functioning well, and the small group of people in authority are connected with the realities of their marketplace. It is an equally dangerous dynamic where the organization is no longer synchronized with its environment and leaders are part of the problem.

Research in Motion (RIM), makers of the BlackBerry mobile device, are a very top-heavy organization with a hierarchy dominated by just two men. Mike Lazaridis and Jim Balsillie serve as both the company's co-CEOs and co-chairmen. Investors don't like the concentration of power in two people inside the company, but mainly they don't like RIM's failure to adapt as fast as their competitors.

In June 2011, an anonymous open letter from a senior employee appeared in various news outlets. It argued that the culture of the company no longer allowed critics to speak openly for fear of having their careers damaged. The employee describes a company out of touch with what consumers want and with what developers want, who make the software for the devices. According to the employee, there is far too much attention paid to what networks ask for and far too little on what users would really appreciate. Making changes for the wrong audience has slowed down and distorted efforts to adapt to the needs of the market.

Back in 2007, the situation seemed very different at RIM head-quarters in Waterloo, Ontario. Back then its CEO could dismiss the 'vanishingly small' success Apple had in the business world, and reject suggestions that the Californian products would ever be any kind of threat. Joint CEO Lazaridis did take time to describe the iPhone virtual keyboard as 'severely limited'. But he still started work on a touch screen competitor.

The problem was that the iPhone killer didn't arrive in 2007. Or 2008. It didn't yet seem a disaster in sales terms. Apple had grabbed over 10 per cent of the smartphone market in only a couple of years but the BlackBerry still had 42 per cent of all sales. By 2009, it was more of a problem. Only a couple of percentage points down but still no product to compete with Apple who had doubled its market share to 20 per cent, one in five smartphones sold.

Lazaridis didn't recognize that people loving their iPhones was a threat. Corporations had invested in BlackBerries but the gleaming Apple product was already more desirable. Each year brought a brand-new iPhone with new features and ever more beautiful design. Each year, the iPhone's serious business credentials grew more impressive, closer and closer to the main reason the BlackBerry kept selling so many handsets.

It was hard to recognize the problem because inside RIM, there were plenty of reasons to think it wasn't that serious. In 2008, it had been named the world's fastest-growing company, managing 84 per cent growth despite the recession. Each year including 2011, sales and profits grew. The problems that were glaring outside RIM could not be seen at the top.

It must have been an awful shock for Lazaridis and Balsillie to realize, in May 2011, that BlackBerry market share had reduced to less than 25 per cent. It had been overtaken by Google and Apple. It must have been made worse on 10 October 2011 when BlackBerry email stopped working, but it was so very much worse when it still wasn't working three days later. This was the worst outage in BlackBerry history: on the week iPhone's latest phone was launched with over four million sold in those same three days.

Even before the problems, RIM had announced that it would miss its 2012 earnings by hundreds of millions of dollars. Its two CEOs had to admit that the Playbook, its competitor to the Apple iPad, was selling slowly. They had to confess the company had been too slow in releasing new smartphones. They argued few companies could have survived the competitive turmoil and that it was having two people at the top of the company that made it all possible. But they still announced job losses.

Part of the problem was the disappointing quality and features of recent products. Their Playbook tablet computer required a BlackBerry phone to work, without which it was useless. It arrived without support from developers. Even the most basic software was missing. Networks failed to support it because it was so obviously not ready to compete.

The disappointing quality and features were a result of failure to adapt at the top of the company. The joint leadership team was somehow unable to fully recognize the nature of adaptation required. Analysts told them that they had to move faster, but they didn't. One of their CEOs even stormed out of an interview when a journalist dared criticize him.

They did not even appear to understand the nature of the adaptation required. And they certainly were not able to explain what they were doing clearly enough for anyone to follow. As in the following example where CEO Balsillie was asked about his reaction to the iPhone: 'My experience is one person may be make a baby in nine months, nine people can't make a baby in one month. But who knows may be some natural constructs can be shifted and we'll have to revive those views and they can shorten these realities.'

No employee, partner or customer would be able to follow that kind of muddled thinking. It goes deeper than being bad at communication. It is exactly what would be expected if leadership no longer understand what needs to be done. In their minds, BlackBerry is still the fastest-growing, record-breaking, industry-changing, celebrity-endorsed superhero. And, so far, they have been unable to get beyond that outdated self-image.

It's possible that they will find a way of getting back ahead of the competition. They have bought a new operating system and a new company to design the way their phones look and feel. But unless the leadership releases its stranglehold on what is considered acceptable and unacceptable thought, renewal will not happen. In just five years, they have lost more than half of their market share, many of their most talented employees, and almost all of their credibility.

All these problems have the same cause. The dominance of a couple of people over the way everyone else is allowed to think and act. It's the opposite of what is necessary for effective adaptation. For employees happy to do nothing but obey orders, working conditions were quite good. For employees who wanted to do something to help the company adapt successfully to new challenges, career prospects were poor. The people at the top rejected challenges to their world view, and that encouraged sycophants and sociopaths at all levels to repress alternative opinions:

> If I could only tell Mike, Jim and the rest of the C*O crowd one thing, it would be this: stop keeping the incredible pool of smart, talented and capable people handcuffed by poorly thought through process. It's destroying the company, and destroying those of us that have to manage it. Being able to move quickly and innovate is what will save the company, and that goes completely opposite all our process.

This view of the company was not uncommon. The people always know what is wrong. It was no surprise to them that the company had problems or that the lack of a touch screen phone would hurt them more than the lack of a keyboard would hurt Apple. It was not a shock to employees that revenue, market share and profit fell so steeply. But it was painful for them to watch the company they loved fail to adapt.

The domination of muddled thinking from the top down, where just a few minds are preventing others' ideas from being heard, can be reversed. One form of reversal is for the people at the top to be replaced, at which point they can open up, and clarify conversations and thinking. Another form of reversal is for some small group, lower down the organization, or even outside the organization, to successfully change the majority view.

In Africa during 2003, nearly 8,000 miles away from the fast-growing manufacturer of the BlackBerry phone, a small group started something that changed the majority view throughout Kenya and the world. One strand of thinking began in England where Nick Hughes, an employee at Vodafone, wondered whether he could adapt mobile phone technology to make mobile banking popular in Kenya.

Nick found a clever way of attracting investment from his government and his company to find an answer to his question. He also found an ally in Susie Lonie, a mobile banking specialist with a degree in engineering who had worked at Vodafone since 2001. She flew to Kenya in 2005 for a three-month business trip and stayed for another three years. In that time, the service known as M-Pesa had grown to three million customers.

The pilot team included Sagentia, a small company from Cambridge, England. They designed the original software, processes, and provided support during the pilot and after launch. They were on call 24 hours a day in the early months of operation correcting mistakes and dealing with the challenges of rapid growth in usage. If what was intended before the project began had been delivered it would have failed, but it didn't.

The key to adaptive success was a willingness to think together with local people working for Safaricom, the Kenyan company in which Vodafone had a 35 per cent interest. One of the original ideas was to create a tool for repayment of micro-finance loans. This idea was adapted into a more universal service that allowed people to transfer money to other people without going through a bank account. M-Pesa found popularity in Kenya's cash-based economy because it enhanced what already worked.

Thinking together with Kenyan employees and Kenyan customers is what made the difference, because it allowed the team to understand what kind of service would fit well enough to be embraced. That applied to the way prepaid phones can be used to move money. It applied to keeping the system as beautifully simple as possible. Just as importantly it applied to the market-ing campaign 'Send money home' that emphasized how service would support something of huge importance in Kenyan society: home.

They also emphasized the desire of many Kenyans to avoid dealing with organizations seen as bureaucratic, slow, or even corrupt. The new service did not require a bank account, therefore no banks. And it did not require a fixed line, therefore no involvement with the old monopolies. Government regulation covering mobile commerce and banking was forced to follow on after people had already created a market.

The service now has 14 million users. Parents use it to pay school fees and send pocket money to their children. It's used to pay for drinks at clubs where no other system could be guaranteed secure. The electronic cash cannot be easily stolen and has found uses on public transport, and has since expanded into a savings account that pays interest on deposits over 1 Kenyan shilling (1 US cent). It's even used as a verb.

Most attempts at adaptation are a kind of trial and error process that guesses what seems to be the best choice based on the past and then forms habits around what has been done most often. For almost all people, the decision to follow a certain pattern of actions is made very rapidly with little understanding of other players' motives.

In 2010, a fascinating experiment was carried out with two groups of players in a business game. Undergraduate and post-graduate MBA students were recruited from the University of Virginia. They were all paid $10 for participating and could then earn cash according to how well they did at the game. Two partners played parts of two newspaper sellers sharing stock to reduce the problems of ordering too much or too little.

The aim of the game was to choose an order quantity that was most likely to be accurate. If one player ordered too few news-papers while the other player ordered too many, then excess newspapers were transferred between them. Customer demand was randomly generated. Players were told whether, and how many, books had been transferred. They were also told about their local costs, revenue and decision history. Thirty rounds of the game were played over about an hour.

The researchers looked for three different kinds of decision making that had been found in other research. Players might learn from experience, they might figure out a rational model of what would happen, or they might combine both methods in a sophisticated form of forward thinking.

It turned out that not one single player made all decisions based on a forward-looking model of what should happen. Almost all players (95 per cent) did not use any forward-thinking model to guide their actions; instead they responded to the first few results and then stayed locked in to the same pattern until the end of the game. Only a small group (5 per cent) mixed both learning and a rational model, and this unusual group made the mistake of assuming that their partners would also be forward-thinking.

So we have the vast majority proceeding with no plan, adjusting only briefly to early experiences. And we have the small minority capable of planning four moves ahead yet most likely to assume the vast majority share their forward thinking, so reducing the effectiveness of their plan.

This appears a common pattern of collective thinking. Most people lock on to a particular course of action, they make their minds up early and fail to adapt to evidence that their choices are wrong. As a result, only a small proportion of most people's experiences lead to new learning.

Minds are the starting point for adaptation. However shallow or deep the adaptation is, whether the adaptation is effective, or ineffective, the brain issues orders to the rest of the body. Sometimes actions are taken after considering a wide range of possible actions. Most often, a quick and dirty match is made between actions and what the brain thinks is happening. People may not even know their reasons for what they have done.

Forward-looking planners are confused if they assume other people think much like them. The ability to think several moves ahead is constrained by inability to empathize with a world populated by those who do not think several moves ahead. Only if they change assumptions will their plans be more likely to shape real-world events.

Most of us can benefit if we keep an open mind to evidence about the effectiveness of our actions. We may find our actions are not working quite as we had intended. There may be un-intended consequences that are better or worse than we had hoped. Understanding more about the gap between intention and reality can help us adapt more effectively to events and situations.

When communication breaks down, our collective ability to adapt is reduced. Since we can't share information we find it harder to recognize the need to adapt. Even when we recognize it, it's difficult to openly agree about the kind of adaptation that is necessary. And, for reasons of mutual incomprehension any comprehensive action is made much less likely.

The nature of the problem may seem obvious to many of those involved. The problem is that those who want to collaborate still lack the insights into others' behaviours sufficient to get people thinking and working together. The result can be a state of bewilderment, where even well-meaning people keep misunder-standing each other's arguments.

The problem is made worse if other players play without good intentions because extreme positioning and prejudice become habitual. Players do a little learning at the beginning of their experience with a game and then get stuck in the same patterns without considering any evidence that their actions are counter-productive or mutually unhelpful.

The US budgetary crisis of 2011 is a powerful example of a collapse in mutual comprehension and trust that stopped people thinking effectively as a group. Nearly everyone agreed that US debt was too high. Almost everyone agreed that the US should continue to pay the interest on its debts. And a majority agreed that in the long run, the balance of taxes and spending should change to prevent US debt becoming unsustainable.

Yet the various political parties could not agree on how this should be accomplished. Such disagreement is not necessarily damaging; effective adaptation requires a wide range of possi-bilities. Consensus that is too easy creates the risk of considering alternatives that are too few or too similar. The damaging part of the fight over the US debt ceiling was that it was fought without trying to listen to each other.

This kind of ineffective collective thinking can seem zombie-like in its behaviour. It can be slow moving, cannibalistic and undead in the way it keeps on moving even when it does no good. There are zombie ideas that stagger around without any significant support. They consume resources that are needed by healthy ideas. They infect living ideas leaving them unable to take care of themselves.

In 2009, as an imaginative experiment, a small team of mathe-maticians at the University of Ottawa became the first to examine what might happen to humans in the case of a zombie attack. They gave their zombies all the traditional characteristics from popular movies, and built a model of their likely expansion. They found that zombies will take over unless humans attack them rapidly, overcoming them before they can recover. So it is with zombie behaviour: it must be fought against.

Improving collective ability to think is helpful to effective adaptation. This often involves challenging dominant thinking that has led to an undesirable situation.

The women's movement in Liberia succeeded in altering unhelpful patterns of behaviour that had led to the deaths of 250,000 people. Concentration of power at the top of the makers of the BlackBerry phone prevented rapid adaptation of thinking to transcend the efforts of competitors at Google and Apple. And mutual incomprehension across the political divide slowed down efforts to find an effective set of adaptations to move beyond the great stagnation to a great renewal.

It's not always easy to understand the exact kind of adaptation required to move to a winning position. Efforts to adapt benefit from getting people thinking better together, as a social group. First, because success in thinking together increases the collective intelligence, the total brainpower, applied to the problem. And second, because any enlightenment is shared as a group. Those involved understand what has to be done, making acts of adaptation more likely to succeed.

Start by looking at how people think. Explore the way they reach decisions, examine where information comes from, and how they share their opinions. If you investigate how people think together, you can find creative ways to improve how they think together.

Rule

11

Get a kick-ass partner

The Nazi Zombie game published by Activision came about by accident. It was released in 2008 as a mini-game featured in the fifth instalment of the hugely successful Call of Duty series. It was developed by software engineers working for Treyarch, a subsidiary of Activision founded in 1996 and located in Santa Monica, California. They were responsible for the whole game and ended up adding the mini-game which became a significant success in its own right.

It came about when one developer, Jessie Snyder, and the lead level designer, Jason McCord, were working on Call of Duty: World at War. They were trying to come up with some cool extras. One idea was an impressive end sequence where the player would be trapped in a German bunker facing waves of American troops coming up the beaches of Normandy. Later, in a separate project they added artificial intelligence to some dazed Japanese soldiers who reminded several people of zombies.

Jessie came up with the idea of developing some kind of 'Tower Defence' game in which players would seek to survive each wave of attacks and then use points to buy weapons. These games already existed for casual gamers online, which suggested a proven market.

In addition, he wanted to develop a model for extra content that had been seen in a racing game – Project Gotham 2 – where the mini-game was eventually split into its own franchise. He saw how it might provide additional revenue and a place where developers could play with more extreme ideas without directly affecting the core of an existing franchise. And when he finished he had his epiphany, 'Zombie Nazis!'

What happens next is instructive. Jessie rushed to one of the producers to pitch his fantastic idea. He explained the Tower Defence game idea, the way they could reuse the zombie-like animations and the existing engine to deliver the full interactive, intense first-person vision. The producer wasn't impressed. The producer said it would take too much time and too much money. The producer said it didn't fit, would be too camp and a huge risk. The producer began work on a non-zombie mini-game of his own.

Fortunately for Activision, Jessie continued to share it with other people on the team who had played tower defence games on other game networks like WarCraft. Encouraged by the response, he created a rough prototype of the game and showed it off to a few people. The reaction was good and the creative director gave him permission to continue working. The game the producer was working on was cut because of a lack of resources while Jessie and one programmer worked on Zombies in their spare time and at weekends.

The game continued to be helped along at a grass-roots level by other developers, animators, artists who were enthused by what had been achieved. It was becoming a labour of love for many people in the company. It got to a point where it was fully functional but full of bugs, too slow and unbalanced. The two men at the core of this hobby development were exhausted and overscheduled on the main game release. Just at the point that it looked doomed, senior management stepped in to give Zombies the resources it needed. A genius games designer called Mike Denny was assigned to fix the flaws and turn it into the polished, awesome game it became on release.

Jessie was proved right about the game's popularity and function at a sandbox, a place to play with new ideas, within Treyarch. The Fourth Call of Duty sold over 11 million copies with many players and reviewers describing the Zombie maps as the best part of the game. Three more maps were available in the sixth Call of Duty while five more maps have sold more than 18 million copies as part of downloadable content. It is a significant part of the $1.8 billion online revenue the company generates.

Subsequent events underline the value of multiplying partners and opportunities to adapt. Sharing the franchise between different game studios, teams and countries encouraged different approaches to be used naturally. It also encouraged creative competition between those involved. Whose adaptation of the franchise would be loved the most by fans? Who would receive the best industry reviews? Who could sell the most copies? Or find ways of increasing income? Who would do the coolest stuff?

If you can engage the love of people for doing extraordinary work, they can look to adapt to objectives or dreams that go far beyond expectations in any given industry or nation. Adaptation is not a one-shot-change-or-die proposition. Just as for the ants we encountered early in our journey, great ideas, breakthrough innovations may happen very slowly or incrementally over months, years or centuries. And they may invite external ridicule, or even require the impetus of external ridicule to make the final leap.

Spiderman the musical was a $75 million flop. Financed by Bono, the rest of U2, with Julie Taymor, the genius behind *Lion King* the musical, as director, the production aimed to change the face of musical theatre. The group got involved after Andrew Lloyd Webber joked rock musicians had left him without competition for 25 years.

Events appeared to conspire against them. The group's original producer died after a stroke just as they gathered to sign contracts. Undeterred, they pressed on, leaving artistic decisions to Taymor who appeared focused entirely on making the show a unique artistic spectacle with little or no interest in budgets or timescales.

Painstaking attention to detail can be exactly that: a willingness to pay attention to every detail that is painful to others who do not share that desire for perfection. The production was due to start rehearsals in 2007 but did not start until 2009. There were delays due to escalating costs and time taken to raise additional funds. Further delays were caused by the challenges of stunts needed to bring a web-slinging superhero to life.

To live with it or not to live with it, that is the question. To get over it or not get over it, that is the question. To sacrifice the vision or to try to deliver it regardless of shorter-term costs and considerations, these are the questions that guide efforts of groups. And in the case of Taymor she had already answered the questions with perfectionists' answers. Only the best would do.

The show was rescheduled to open in February 2010. It was then delayed another 10 months to December 2010 to find more money. And still rewrites of dialogue continued, new songs were written, whole scenes added, cut and added and cut again. The opening was delayed again to March 2011 so the director could create a new ending. New writers and composers were drafted in to help improve certain aspects of the music and script. And in a dramatic shift, Taymor was no longer in charge of the production show and left.

At last, in March 2011 the previews to the show started before being shut down again. Before this the stunt actor playing Spiderman suffered injuries when he fell more than 20 feet. He crashed through the stage before landing in the orchestra pit. Another four people had been injured during rehearsals and preview performances.

Press verdicts following previews didn't seem to help. General coverage described it as visually stunning despite technical malfunctions through the performance. While the theatre critics queued up like super villains to throw various pumpkin-shaped bombs, lightning bolts and handfuls of sand in the faces of all involved. The first version of the show was described as among the worst shows ever worthy of an F+. The second version got an average score of C+ but was damned for being better but boring.

The show had improved dramatically. And the public was remarkably willing to buy full-price tickets to watch sold-out preview performances. They were able to accept that there would be technical problems. They seemed drawn to the whole grandeur of vision and relentless commitment displayed by all those involved. They were involved in something historic, something above the humdrum and the already clinically flawless.

As a result, it was bringing in more than $1.5 million a week during the longest preview period in history with 182 preview performances. It became one of the biggest money earners in Broadway history before it even opened. Upon finally opening on 15 June 2011, it went from being described as incoherent, joyless and deranged to receiving praise for awesome images, electrifying moments, exhilarating themes, daring and exuberance. They don't say it's great but it's progress.

Nine years of work. One hundred and eight months of changes big and small. Thirty nine thousand four hundred and twenty days of trying and failing and trying and failing and trying again. The team still believe the show is only 90 per cent complete as it continues to adapt in response to audience feedback and reviews.

Instructively, the spontaneous ad-libbed jokes from Patrick Page, the actor playing the Green Goblin, have been written into the show along with increased stage time for him and his character. The show is still trying to learn, still adapting, audiences like it a lot, and may yet arrive at success beyond the already considerable box office takings.

The already legendary production has already been immortalized in a tribute comedy musical entitled *The Legend of Julie Taymor, or the Musical That Killed Everybody*, with the director shown as an ego-driven crazy woman who sleeps with the theatre owner and kills a man with her bare hands. It has become shorthand for budget and creative excess while at the same time becoming famous for just never giving up.

It's similar to the resilience displayed by Apple in their constant improvements of great ideas that didn't work (at first), or the relentless chassis and team adaptation of Red Bull in pursuit of Formula One championships. But it also illustrates the dangers and long timescales of trying to make something work through just one source of creative judgement.

By contrast, working in the Activision way allows multiple teams to try in *different ways* to find ways of playing a winning game. If Jessie, our hero of the Nazi Zombie mini-game, had not been able to experiment the organization would have been stuck with obvious game features constrained by past releases of the franchise. Adaptation is rarely helped along by choosing winners, particularly at the beginning. And, it's always the beginning.

Adaptation is helped by having a kick-ass partner. It helps in the process of thinking better together in general, and really helps when exploring the practical demands of any necessary adaptation. Having a close working relationship between people with diverse skills and talents increases adaptation effectiveness.

Part

3

Adapt as necessary

After recognizing the need to adapt, and figuring out what kind of adaptation is needed, the next step is actually making the changes necessary. This is a blend of doing what is necessary, getting other people to get involved with you, and focusing effort on what changes the nature of the game being played.

All of the rules discussed in this book look at all three steps to adaptation and all three are necessary to developing a culture that can adapt repeatedly to new opportunities and problems. The goal is not any particular destination. There are no single, unchanging answers that work for ever because our situation, needs and desires keep changing.

Nothing is fixed. Our intelligence can increase or decrease. Our collective ability to think and act has continued to transform throughout human existence. This is the deep and enduring lesson. No single answer will suffice for all seasons; instead our questions offer us the best chance of responding to the needs of the time.

Adaptability is intelligence. It can be the ability to adapt rapidly and gracefully to small changes in structure or process at the workplace. It can be the ability to gain insight from anywhere and respond by enhancing the state of the art in anything. It's the story of organizations like Nike that sends its designers to where sport is played and provokes innovative new materials. It's the story of insurgents in Iraq and Afghanistan that out-adapt traditional hierarchy. It's the story of baseball teams in Oakland, and football teams in Holland.

Some individuals and groups are very good at winning an existing game, changing their behaviour if necessary to be best at playing. We'll meet billionaires who started as street vendors, and games designers who create what customers want to buy.

The higher skill is to figure out how to organize so that the game itself is better for as many people as possible. We should seek enlightenment about the adaptation required but also the need for perpetual adaptation. Decay necessitates renewal. This great stagnation is part of a complex game from which we may seek a better way of creating and sharing that can take us through the next hundred years.

Rule
12
Never grow up

HP is getting out of computers. Ten years after buying Compaq with the express goal of becoming the world's number-one personal computer company, its new CEO has decided to sell. It spent $25 billion on the acquisition and fought a painful legal battle against the son of one of the founders to enforce the will of CEO Fiorina. And now it's selling again.

Organizations get old. They grow up. They lose that edginess that gave them a competitive edge when they were start-ups. Most corporations lose the edge that led to their eventual success. The original entrepreneurs are replaced with professional managers who are given the responsibility to sort out the mess left behind by the amateurs who gave the company life.

At HP, the crisis of youthful disorganization has long since been replaced by dysfunctional middle age. It's all so wasteful. It's so adult. It's so painfully realistic leaving little room for joy, courage or humour. There's the political fighting and the macho (male and female) posturing. It's an unhealthy menu of the apathetic, the amoral and the incompetent.

And just when they were on track again, with a strategy and leader that made sense, the board found a reason to fire the CEO. It's not that he was perfect but at least he understood the nature of his industry and company. He had invested $1.2 billion in the remains of Palm Inc, the one-time smart device market leaders, and was about to start delivering products that might (eventually) compete with Apple the market leader.

On paper, they do everything right at HP. They have the layers of traditional hierarchy. They benchmark. They have staff surveys. Yet they are dominated by heavy duty, top-down leadership and, every now and then, thrown into further confusion by an accident-prone board.

The board of directors might respond that they have been forced to make changes to survive. It's necessary, they might say, to shake things up from time to time in order to bring new perspectives into the company.

It is because HP veers between mid-life crisis and middle-aged complacency that it looks outside for renewal. Leaders seek the secret of perpetual youth and vigour via acquisition. Rather than spending time with their own people they prefer to spend huge sums of money on acquiring the success of others.

This has led the board to look outside the industry for a new CEO. Something they did with Carly Fiorina who forced through the purchase of Compaq. And the latest HP CEO, fresh from SAP, the German software company, looks outside the company for answers to growth that make him less uncomfortable with his lack of knowledge. It is so very rare that a CEO is comfortable, child-like with learning what is necessary from the people who do the work and know the answers.

Instead, many leaders follow the patterns in the career playbook that got the job in the first place. So, HP under ex-CEO Hurd did hardware and software because that's what Hurd did at his previous employer NCR. And now, under Apotheker HP tried to create software for other corporations because that's what he did at his previous employer SAP.

He risked destroying the best of what existed before him in order to replace it with expensive acquisitions he understands. Which is why, before this book was even completed; he had been fired after just 12 months. He has been replaced with Meg Whitman, ex-CEO of eBay who will do what she has already done, move to software as a service, or hopefully, start again.

This approach to adapting requires the organization to adapt to the skills and knowledge of the leader. Anything that does not fit is cut off. Anything that is needed is bought and retrofitted in a Frankenstein-style experiment that risks bringing an unhappy, unloved hybrid monster to life.

The most successfully adaptive companies are those that **never grow up**. Instead of buying into the notion that they must become old and boring like their competitors, they stay for ever young. Some remain fun-loving, curiosity-driven rock stars long after their peer group have gained grey hairs, suits and a clichéd vocabulary of nauseating corporate speak. They refuse the down-sides of maturity and the longer they refuse the more successful they remain. Growth is not something adults do.

Pretty much all the poster boy billionaires start out that way. Microsoft people played practical jokes, drank, partied and coded for days on end. They wanted to put a computer on every desk. They were genius hobbyists obsessed with making their dreams reality. Here's an example of Microsoft pranksters at work:

> The first Bouncy Ball war was an accident. We had a ping pong table, and it was in use in the lobby of the Northup building one evening, perhaps 8pm [...] As one of the ping pong players went up for a big smash, 500 bouncy balls were dumped from the landing above. For several long seconds, nobody understood what had happened. Then everybody did. Soon a dozen people

were involved, occasionally traitorously switching between below, where most of the ammunition was, but with virtually no defenses, and above, with good defenses but little ammo. People wandered through and immediately got caught up in the action. Everybody had a great time.

Google has also pulled off several famous April Fool's Days hoaxes. It's first in 2000, the MentalPlex, asked users to try to send a mental image of what they wanted to find. An animation on the screen would then display a random message indicating an error message including the classic: 'Error 001: Weak or no signal detected. Upgrade transmitter and retry.' Google has since featured PigeonRank, a method of improving search results with trained birds, advertisements for fictitious job openings on the moon, and scratch-and-sniff functionality.

These pranks indicate a kind of excess creativity and enthusiasm that cannot be contained by the day-to-day work. They suggest the kind of energy and thinking needed in a culture that is capable of rapid adaptation. They also serve as a way of keeping the organization young. They help people relax. Playing shakes off the pressures of the day and overcomes some of the unhelpful formality that increases over time.

Sending people into the world to play appears wasteful to many leaders, who are only comfortable when workers are doing what they understand and can control. Yet, the most adaptive organizations recognize that playfully interacting with the real world reveals new answers.

Nike's first shoes were a fusion of a love for athletics and a waffle iron filled with rubber. They organize around individual sports to increase their stimulus to adapt. Instead of just designing a general shoe, they are prompted to design a specific shoe adapted to a particular need.

Back in 2008, one of their designers, Shane Kohatsu, travelled to China just to look at how basketball was played there. He noticed that street ballers opted for really durable footwear like hiking boots to cope with the demands of hard concrete and high temperatures. He watched the players, he played with them and designed a new fabric, Hyperfuse, that could cope with the heat and the harsh conditions. Never grow up.

Rule
13
Hierarchy is fossil fuel

'This year we at Sony have been flooded, we've been flattened, we've been hacked and we've been singed [...] but the summer of our discontent is behind us,' declared the Sony CEO, Sir Howard Stringer.

In 2011, this giant, multi-billion-dollar electronics and entertainment corporation had been beset by problems. There was natural disaster, unnatural competition and social unrest. Leaderless, invisible attackers outwitted Sony's traditional hierarchy. Its ability to move from noticing to reacting was exposed as it struggled to see the problems or adapt to them.

Traditional hierarchy has problems at multiple levels. Traditional top-down heavy hierarchy has its people locked in boxes of its own creation. Traditional we-all-know-our-place hierarchy never knows whose job it is but always whose job it's not. It's the dominant form of organization despite its problems, costs, frictions and inefficiencies. As a structure it resists learning and institutionalizes self-interested behaviour. Why do your best when your best is likely to cause you problems?

Traditional industrial-age hierarchy was a revolution of sorts when it emerged in its bureaucratic brilliance from the stultifying constraints of leadership-by-birth aristocratic privilege. The old way held back the best and brightest with visible and invisible chains. The new way suggested influence and reward based on merit. And if not merit then on position where professional qualification was the key to each floor of the organizational chart.

Generations have invested their working lives in such hierarchies. Bureaucratic rules have structured the working days, lunch hours and toilet breaks of billions. Layers of managers piled up between boardroom and frontline. Work lives defined in theoretical job descriptions presented by human resources professionals with the best of intentions. Visions, values, missions and behaviours attempt to align intentions with actions and aspirations with events.

And since strategy and structure are so very interdependent, the hierarchy gets in the way of adaptation to circumstance. As a result, change internally in response to change externally can be pitifully, painfully slow. Groups adapt at very different speeds. The difference in speed depends on how effectively their cultures encourage or discourage autonomous behaviour.

Sony struggled with exactly this kind of adaptive challenge. In 2011, a relatively small number of US executives among their 168,000 employees decided to file a lawsuit against one individual – George Hotz, a 21-year-old American from New Jersey.

The company was unhappy that George – voted one of the top overachievers in the world – had outwitted them. He had publicly published his method of getting past the security on the Sony games console – the PS3.

The security had been set in place to stop people using the games console in any new ways that Sony did not directly approve. Its main benefit to Sony was to encourage sales of new games by stopping pirated games and old games for previous games consoles working.

Sony's system had the reputation of being unhackable but, as George explained to the BBC, 'Nothing is unhackable.' It was a remarkable achievement that required, according to our young genius, just five weeks. He managed to use hardware to create an insecurity in the PS3 and use that insecurity as a door into the rest of the system. The technique meant he could make the PS3 do pretty much anything he wanted including running other operating systems and homemade games.

Why did he do it? Curiosity. And a belief in open systems. Sony opted to respond to his idealistic interest by taking him to court.

Well, perhaps in the not-too-distant past, expectation would be for a corporate lawsuit aimed at an individual without billions at his disposal to achieve its aim of scaring him into compliance. He was alone without corporate back-up. Those without institutional support are easier to crush, so the reasoning goes.

The traditional imbalance of power is something that has encouraged lawsuits being directed at the relatively weak. Corporations have aimed their legal might at grandmothers whose grandchildren have downloaded music and entrepreneurial innovators who have threatened the complacency of markets. But not this time.

Let's see. There was the blog he started about the legal attacks, the professor at Craig Mellon University who issued a statement supporting Hotz's right to free speech, and the rap video George posted on YouTube with the defiant lines:

> Those that can't do bring suits,
>
> Cry to your Uncle Sam to settle disputes,
>
> But shit man, they're a corporation,
>
> And I'm a personification of freedom for all.

What did Sony do this time? Well, somebody decided to force You-Tube, through the law courts, to hand over the details of anyone who had *viewed* George's videos about the hacking of the PS3. It was a move that was excessive. It was also counterproductive.

Its heavy-handed actions increased further the number of people likely to be unhappy with its actions. And some of those people were supporters of Anonymous, a leaderless movement that uses internet attacks to support its views concerning freedom on the web and elsewhere.

Attracting their attention seems unwise. It is difficult to fight a group without a leader. It was particularly difficult for Sony to win against people not playing by traditional rules or for the same corporate objectives. Those involved didn't have a profit motive. They were not constrained by hierarchy and could move in a multitude of ways, faster, and in more unpredictably, creative ways than Sony could manage.

The emblem of Anonymous is a headless figure symbolizing their structure as having no one leader. They are a group that emerged in 2003 from discussions on the web-image-sharing board 4chan. They discussed the idea of people working together in an anarchic, distributed global brain.

They imagined a decentralized community acting together in pursuit of loosely agreed shared objectives. This form of organization proved to be remarkably fluid since it depended not on hierarchy but upon more-or-less shared beliefs to determine the 'who, what, how, where and when' of their actions.

Their shared beliefs include freedom of speech offline and online. These beliefs guide discussion about what, and who, should be defended or attacked. Tactics, methods and targets are discussed and debated yet final actions are left to the individual. When someone does something in the name of Anonymous they attribute the action to the movement. They do not want recognition individually.

The ideals of Anonymous started with something akin to hedonistic, personal freedom yet in time this evolved into an interest in protecting the rights of others – even society. They added the Church of Scientology to the list of targets in 2008, seeking to highlight what they called 'exploitation of church members'. By 2009, they had turned their collective attention to the fight for free and fair Iranian elections. They created a support website called Anonymous Iran that allows communication despite government efforts to shut it down.

In 2010, reawakened – in its terms – by attacks on freedom, Anonymous started attacks in retaliation for what it saw as oppression of Julian Assange, the founder of the wikileaks investigative news website. They have supported the revolutions in Egypt, Syria, Libya and in other countries throughout the Middle East. They have disrupted government websites in all these areas to draw attention to attacks on freedom.

And so when George Hotz was threatened, Anonymous also attacked Sony's PS3 network. Not because he asked or because he was involved. But because the collective mind of Anonymous – the individuals who work loosely together – felt that his treatment was unfair and threatened freedom beyond a single individual.

The attacks by Anonymous from April 2011 demonstrated security vulnerabilities in Sony's network. They gave someone the opportunity to copy 77 million user names which forced Sony to stop service to gamers for two months. The service disruption hurt its reputation although – as Sony claims – it may have ultimately improved the technology it was using. It has even added 3 million users to the network since the attack.

But their traditional hierarchy made the wrong move at the wrong time. It was an avoidable misstep by one part of the hierarchy made without thought for the consquences. The collective mind of Sony was not engaged with this decision. The decision was made by a small minority without reference to the whole. And the layers of decision making throughout Sony meant that it did not even recognize the seriousness of attacks until days after they had happened. The hierarchy survived but the emergent organizational form thrived.

This is not a defence of or an attack on Anonymous. It is impossible to know exactly what is being done by whom – that is kind of the point. Nor is it an argument that traditional hierarchy is dead. It is not. Instead, you should know that hierarchy is not the only – or the most adaptive – form for structuring human collaboration.

Before Sony managed to bring its network back online, it settled out of court with George Hotz. And the boy-genius is working for Facebook, a company that – so far – understands the limitation of hierarchy and the enhanced adaptability of alternatives.

Rule
14
Keep the ball

Oakland Athletics have given up the joy of winning for the comfort of consistency. They are the subject of a best-selling book by Michael Lewis and a Hollywood movie starring Brad Pitt. The stars of the book and movie are not the players, or the game. The stars are the general manager, Billy Beane, and his use of measurement.

The standard story is that they have triumphed by applying mathematics to baseball. By measuring carefully, the field of sabermetrics attempts to determine the real value of a player in the past and predict the value of that player in the future. In 2006, Oakland were ranked the fifth best team but paid the 24th lowest wages out of the 30 teams.

The approach, it is claimed, has allowed Oakland to recruit bargain players. They could find players who were undervalued because other managers made their decisions based on myths, not facts. Similar data could also change the way managers organized their teams and the tactics for games. Focusing on defence, not offence, was a typical change.

This all makes sense until you look at the results. They have not won enough to reach a World Series since 1990. Not even in 2002, when they won 20 games in a row to qualify for the play-offs, were they able to get beyond the semi-final first round.

Since 2006, the number of wins has been 93, 76, 75 and 75, 81, and 88. Four years, no play-off in sight.

Since 1998, when Beane became general manager of Oaklands, the New York Yankees have won the World Series four times and been in the finals twice more. Nine teams out of thirty have won the World Series, but not Oakland. They have adapted into a game-winning team despite relatively low spending. Yet Beane and the owners have been unable to transcend their situation sufficiently to win championships instead of games.

Compare this to what's happening over at the University of Oregon. Here their team had a pitiful record in college football. Their first one hundred years brought them limited success. This started to change from 1995 when Mike Bellotti took over as head coach. In his very first year, he led the team to a 9–3 record and competed in the Cotton Bowl Classic. Over the course of his tenure, the team was selected for 12 bowls out of 14 attempts and only once did they lose more games than they won.

In 1996 the founder of Nike, Phil Knight, offered Belotti his help. The coach asked for somewhere to practise indoors, so Knight paid for one to be designed, built and maintained. Since then he has spent more than $300 million on additional facilities, which all helped, but that wasn't the whole story. It tells us something, that an existing game can be adapted dramatically if it can attract additional resources from outside the game.

This is something that Phil Knight understands. He has been part of a 50-year process of adapting the humble plimsoll into a gliding, air-cushioned, dream factory. Originality attracts attention. Attention provokes action. Actions can change the winners of the game or the nature of the game. Knight asked his designers 'How can we help attract better students and better student-athletes?' Their answer included making them look cool:

Blocky, standard letters became sleek, modern fonts. Wings on the shoulders? Diamond designs on the knees? Silver shoes worn at Southern Cal? 'Nothing,' Nike creative director Todd Van Horne said, 'is off the table.' The paint for the dark green helmets was made with glass beads and cost $2,400 a gallon. There were fall fashion shows.

This is interesting. The uniform changes the game because teenagers considering where to play football are more likely to want to look cool while they're doing it. Their stars talk about how their love for the uniforms encouraged them to move to the backwaters. The style of the uniforms creates a buzz that attracts talent to the team. Talent helps the team to win. The Oregon Ducks are now the number-one ranked team.

Nike's use of style changed the traditional balance of power in US college football because it redirected the flow of talent. Power is produced by a system that works in a particular way. If you change the flow of any system, you can change the outcomes of that system. The change was small, in a sense, the change seemed superficial. First, it was misunderstood, and then after it succeeded it was copied by other teams.

Deep adaptation may appear to produce rapid success but only because it only gains wider acknowledgement after it proves to be successful. It took 15 years for Oregon to become the number-one ranked team from the time that Nike got involved. Over in Europe, a revolution in sport took even longer, starting back at the turn of the century in England and reaching a peak during the 2010 World Cup final in South Africa where Spain became champions.

In 1915, the Ajax football team appointed a new coach from England. Jack Reynolds had not been a star player; he'd won nothing, had not been part of his international team, and had even been described as mediocre. He ended up in Holland after a year managing in Switzerland. He spent the next decade insisting that players of all ages were taught the same tactics and played with the same playing style.

After a brief time managing their city rivals, he returned and won five league titles. He introduced the concept of wingers attacking midfield players on either side who run from defence to attack, along with the practice of keeping the ball, passing simply on the floor until they created an opportunity to score. Thirty-two years after joining the club, including five years as a prisoner of war in Upper Silesia, now a part of Poland, he returned to win a last title before retiring.

One of the players Reynolds coached in that last season was Rinus Michels who became head coach of Ajax nearly 20 years later. Threatened by relegation, he returned to the system of possession and further advanced the idea of players moving fluidly from defence to attack. In part, they needed to adapt their system to cope with the playing style of their star attacking player Johan Cruyff.

Cruyff drifted around the pitch looking for the best space in which to cause problems to the opposition. His team learned to switch positions to cover for his movement, each player obliged to learn the responsibilities of all other players. Each player became a total footballer adept in defence, midfield and attack. It brought them six national championships, three national cups and three consecutive European cups.

With the great Johan involved the whole club learned the importance of creating and using space. The idea kept developing as the players and coaches saw the potential. Cruyff felt that 'simple football is the hardest thing' because of the extensive training required. Using space intelligently necessitated more than creativity. Changing the game needed hours of practice in weaving shapes from simple passing.

Perhaps the ultimate expression of total football has been in Spain with Barcelona. The team recruited Cruyff as a player and employed five previous Ajax men as head coach.

Reynolds, Kovacs and Michels – the coaches who had worked most with the system in Holland – wouldn't live to see the pinnacle of total football with Spain defeating the Dutch team 1–0 in the World Cup final in 2010. With seven players from the all-conquering Barcelona team, they played the patient style introduced to their club from Ajax. Some dispute that this Barcelona style is total football, but the system that has attracted the name tiki-taka is a clear adaptation of the same principles. It has been adapted to the particular skills available, based around a short passing game from back to front. It involves less movement of players, more movement of the ball. Like total football, it mesmerizes the opposition who find themselves without the ball for 70 per cent of the game.

Any system is open to improvement. Any game can be overcome however impossible that seems at first. For Oakland, a new reliance on statistics brought them into a holding pattern that took them ahead of most rivals and delivered value but not trophies. Even the data analysis has been copied by other teams. For Oregon, a century of mediocrity was followed by reaching 12 bowls in 14 years and a number-one position. For Barcelona, 15 long years without European success was followed by three wins in four years.

The most successful adaptors reduce the game down to its fundamental components. This simplified view captures the most important features of the system they are trying to improve. With the most important features identified, it is then possible to reimagine parts of the system and then work to improve them. This is what Cruyff meant when he said playing a simple game is the hardest thing to do.

There is competition inside the game and outside the game. Inside the game, it is possible to work harder, to try to become the best at playing in the way that has become traditional. Only outside the game can new advantages be found that remove traditional constraints. It requires an understanding of deeper patterns; this understanding allows the adaptor to compete outside the game.

Oregon overcame years of prestige of their rivals by focusing on the simple idea of attracting teenagers with cool design. The total football concept brought Ajax and Barcelona repeated European success in part because they compete in the years of preparation before any particular 90-minute game began. They kept the ball and did something with it.

Rule
15
Swerve and swarm

When Li Ka-Shing was just 15, his father died. The teenager was left to support his mother, sister and brother by selling plastic watchbands and belts in 1940s Hong Kong. Born in Chaozhou, Guangdong province on mainland China, his family fled the Japanese army who invaded in 1940.

By the time he became the breadwinner, the three years and eight months of Japanese occupation of Hong Kong had begun. This was a period of chaotic uncertainty. The local currency was forcibly replaced with Military Yen issued without reserves. Hyper-inflation, food rationing, rape, executions and deportations were inflicted upon the population.

Li was set apart by his speed of moving from intuition to action. Within a couple of years he moved into wholesale sales, then rapidly became a general manager by the time he was 19. In 1949, aged 22, he had enough credibility for friends to lend him money to start up his own plastics company. He named it after the Yangtze River to show his belief in how smaller streams of effort can combine with great power. He has made a profit every year since.

Seven years later, he went to Italy and learned to manufacture high-quality plastic flowers. He was always interested in how things worked. He asked questions, and bought used textbooks to increase his knowledge even while an apprentice. He wanted to understand the latest trends so that he could recognize opportunities to adapt his actions and change destiny. He became known as the global 'king of flowers'.

In 1967, with riots causing panic and fear, he made large investments in land, betting that the economy and society were sound and would grow. The result of his bet was a real estate business that by 1971 was more profitable than manufacturing. His company, renamed as Cheung Kong Holdings, was listed on the Hong Kong Stock Exchange in 1972.

His conglomerate expanded to include telecommunications, infrastructure, container ships, porters, retailers and life sciences. By 2011, the group employed nearly a quarter of a million people in 55 countries and is valued at $100 billion. His personal wealth is more than $26 billion. Known in Asia as 'Superman', he is the world's seventh richest person.

Li followed his intuition when he shut down the Rabbit mobile phone service in England after only 20 months at a loss of $183 million. It was a good opportunity overtaken by competitors. He followed his intuition again by founding Orange in 1992 and selling it in 1999 to Mannesmann for $33 billion. As soon as contractually possible, he founded the brand '3' and invested billions in 3G networks his competitors couldn't afford.

Li Ka Shing published his own 12 philosophies including the importance of fighting against adversity with diligence, forming a united front, and competing fairly. Of direct relevance are the following three:

'Observe the market condition and seize up on a good opportunity.'

'Have a creative mentality and a clear view point to eliminate following trends blindly.'

'Take measures according to situations with adaptability, look for multiple opportunities.'

At 5.59 am, no matter how late the previous night, he wakes up and begins to listen to the 6 am news bulletin. This allows him to observe market conditions and then adapt his actions rapidly to take advantage of multiple opportunities. He is the epitome of Hong Kong adaptability.

And yet, the Hong Kong system has not necessarily improved for the poorest of its inhabitants who suffer from the cost of housing kept artificially high by tycoons like Li Ka-Shing. The government auctions new land only occasionally to keep supply low, and when it does it only sells large parcels of land that are out of reach to individual or community groups. Only billionaires need apply and only billionaires ever do.

Shanty towns still exist. In 2010, there were nearly 400,000 shanty structures mostly in the new territories to the north but still more than 2,000 in Kowloon and 4,500 on Hong Kong Island. There are shanty structures on the backstreets and on the rooftops. The Gini coefficient measuring the gap between richest and poorest is the worst in Asia.

In part this is because of the immense wealth but also because there are over one million people who have an income less than half of the median wage. There is no minimum wage, although for 40 per cent there is subsidized social housing. The government here spends only 16 per cent or so of the national income on the social fabric, and so, not surprisingly, there is relatively little for those in the bottom half.

It took a fire in the Shek Kip Mei shanty town for social housing projects to begin in Hong Kong. After 53,000 people were left homeless, the government started to build high-rise tenement blocks that were only a partial advance on what went before. They were more resilient to fires and floods and each apartment had a toilet. They were also very small, perhaps 30 square metres, each housing up to five people although in practice there would often be two families and up to 20 people. The blocks had 500 apartments with rent at the time about $14 a month.

Until recently, the success of Hong Kong was seen to be 'big market, small government' with a belief in few regulations, low tax, and little help in overcoming the problems inherent in any economic system. Now despite growth of 26 per cent over the past seven years, the poor are poorer still, and the rental prices rise ever higher. It has become in the view of many a source of social discontent that risks becoming a crisis.

What works for changing a social system perceived to be unfair? What can be done to alter a social equilibrium that is undesirable, violent or unjust? Part of this is recognition of the problem. When half a million demonstrators assembled on 1 July 2003, Tung Chee Hwa, the highest authority in Hong Kong, was forced to step down.

Similar activity in mainland China includes what are referred to as 'walks' where thousands of people will gather to walk around the building that is central to their unhappiness. In September 2011, in Dalian, to the north east, protests were against a factory making a flammable liquid used in fabric production that also caused cancer. In the same month, in Haining to the east, hundreds protested for three days against pollution.

Unfortunately, while people may recognize the problem they may not see how it is their problem. They can see the problem of overcrowding, or poverty, or pollution, but can convince themselves that it's part of the economic system. They can see the inequality but be reassured that intelligence and contribution explain all the differences between people.

Efforts to increase recognition of the need or possibility for adaptation are valuable. The value of protest can be in dragging eyes towards a particular situation: some campaigns attract willpower to do something if only people knew what; the most valuable protests increase the brainpower applied to understanding the nature of the adaptation required. They encourage better thinking together: emergent thinking.

Back on 13 July 2011, one of the creative minds at Adbusters, a campaigning organization based in Canada, proposed a peaceful protest on Wall Street. Their creative minds include 90,000 people who take part in an online community of global brainstorming. Someone suggested a hashtag on Twitter as a way of discussing the idea. Others created a poster of a dancer on top of a charging bull to advertise a one-day protest on Wall Street using the simple slogan: 'Get money out of politics.'

Using Twitter as an online network was an effective choice. Twitter users like clever wordplay, they like self-organizing, and Western Twitter users had looked upon civil disobedience in Arab nations with an interest approaching envy. People associated with the Anonymous group encouraged others to 'Flood lower Manhattan' and 'Occupy Wall Street'.

And they did. Thousands of people took part in New York. And then Detroit, and Oakland. And Paris, and London. They deliberately adapted from the technique of swerving attacks to one of swarming to occupy a symbolically important place. The following quote by Raimundo Viejo of Pompeu Fabra University in Spain was used in the original blog post by Adbusters, and illustrates the adaptation of tactics: 'Back then our model was to attack the system like a pack of wolves. There was an alpha male, a wolf who led the pack, and those who followed behind. Now the model has evolved. Today we are one big swarm of people.'

The tactic was meant to include incessantly repeating 'one simple demand in a plurality of voices'. It was inspired by the demand made by people in Tahrir Square, Egypt, that President Mubarak should go. The difficulty was that the demands of the occupy protestors were not anywhere close to being as straightforward. Even in the original blog post, the demand for 'Democracy not Corporatocracy' is complex and unclear.

Yet it did get people talking. The media were fascinated by the contrast between famous landmarks and tent villages. The campaign did resonate with people who were not involved directly with protests. The desire to reduce corruption, share wealth and increase opportunity was widespread. Opinion polls suggested that a majority of the USA supported the protestors' feelings about corporate greed and links to politics.

'The whole world is watching,' said one protestor when faced with the prospect of arrest in New York. Whether he knew it or not, 'the world is watching' as a slogan has a history. It was chanted by anti-war protestors outside the Hilton Hotel in Chicago in 1968 during the Democratic National Convention as they were arrested by police. Protestors seek to encourage change by gaining public attention and support. The world was now watching but would it also gain an understanding of what needed to be done for the economic and social systems to be improved?

Understanding what has to be done is a significant step in all deliberate social adaptation. Clarity may not be where adaptation begins, because the answer is rarely known before the question is asked. Even if the originator of the question has their own personal answer, the details will tend to change as more people get involved. Significant change is not possible without mass involvement; mass involvement shifts the answers.

In London, the Occupy movement provoked debate between different sides of the Anglican Church by establishing one of its two encampments outside St Paul's cathedral. The choice of the site was unintentional. The group originally intended pitching tents at the London Stock Exchange but police, acting on an injunction, sealed the entrance. A couple of thousand ended up outside St Paul's Cathedral. They stayed.

On 16 October, the group issued an initial statement that was drafted by around 500 people on the cathedral steps. The group discussed the reasons for their protest until the nine-point statement emerged. It included the view that alternatives to the current economic and political system were needed, that spending cuts were not inevitable, and that structural change was necessary to establish global equality.

The protest did not start with those demands, they emerged. If the changes they seek happen it will be because others join the discussion about those alternatives. Just including the word 'alternative' in mass media broadcasts enlarges the possibilities that received serious discussion. This, in turn, increases the possibility that alternative actions will be taken that are superior to those existing before the protest.

This principle, or mechanism of adaptation, seems to apply more generally than the immediate protests. Attention must be gained in a way that increases efforts to change whatever system is viewed as a problem by protestors. The opportunity to contribute needs to be sufficiently clear or open, to divert energy into remaking social and economic mechanisms.

The opportunity to contribute is more important, especially in the early stages, than the specific set of changes. These can evolve; they may require discussion and amendment in ways that cannot be seen at the start. There has to be room in the plan for possibilities and even compromises that were not understood when those plans were written.

In 1971, workers faced with the closure of the shipyards on the River Clyde rejected the idea of a traditional strike and instead chose to stage what they called a 'work-in'. Everyone continued to complete existing orders, even those who had lost their jobs already. They built ships while working to change government policy and get the support that they needed. From the factory floor to the most senior managers, the idea was to show the world that a spirit of collaboration existed that made the whole shipyard viable. As, Jimmy Reid, the shipyard union leader said:

> We are not going to strike. We are not even having a sit-in strike. Nobody and nothing will come in and nothing will go out without our permission. And there will be no hooliganism, there will be no vandalism, there will be no bevvying [drinking] because the world is watching us, and it is our responsibility to conduct ourselves with responsibility, and with dignity, and with maturity.

He also understood that the 'world is watching' and that understanding informed the creative response of his group. They adapted traditional union tactics as a way of gaining greater public support and of prompting government energy to help them rather than breaking the strike. This was a non-obvious strategy that led to a non-obvious solution.

The right-of-centre government, led by Edward Heath, appeared to want an answer that did not require an increase in unemployment. The creativity of the unions made it easier for various groups to support the union's call for a right to work. After less than a year, a loan was provided to the Clyde shipbuilding industry that survives in various forms today.

Combining swerving, avoiding dominance of the obvious idea, and swarming, to bring mass participation to finding non-obvious answers is powerful. People have long been brought together in seemingly spontaneous ways. Symbolism can reach many people who do not know each other but feel moved by the same cause or objective.

The prevalence of mobile phones is just one more way to organize. Flash mobs, as with silent dancers in London's Liverpool Street

Station or pillow fights in Seattle. Smart mobs are more political, such as the two-minute gay-kiss protest in Barcelona against the Catholic Church's stance on homosexuality. Flash mobs describe groups of up to one hundred young people who all arrive at the same place to cause problems or even loot. Similar tactics were used in London's 2011 riots but also in the efforts to tidy up after the riots. Protests in Moldova, Iran, Tunisia, Egypt and others have all received the sobriquet, the Twitter Revolution.

It's not just protestors who swerve and swarm. McDonald's was in trouble in the 1990s. It had run after global expansion and efficiency responding dismissively to trends and aggressively towards critics. An unimaginative pact with profits came at the cost of understanding what customers wanted to eat and where they wanted to eat.

The start of renewal came from an unexpected place, not from the centre but from about 12,000 miles away in Melbourne, Australia. And the idea didn't really start with a careful corporate analysis of the future needs of its global business. The idea started with a single pot of coffee on the countertop, put there for rush-hour commuters in need of a caffeine fix.

Ann Brown was the franchisee of the McDonald's store that hit upon the idea of adding decent coffee to the menu. It was an unofficial extra. It took six more years before it became a fully recognized part of the McDonald's operation, with a made-to-measure combined store opening in Brisbane in 1999. The adaptation is finally recognized in the 2000 annual report where the CEO, Jack Greenberg, praised the concept that was now in 300 stores. By 2010, there were more than 1,300 locations globally.

At headquarters in Illinois, the focus was on expansion through new stores. Where this proved difficult senior managers turned their attention to an acquisitions binge. In a year, they snapped up a bankrupt eatery chain for $173 million, bought into Pret A

Manger, and bought three chains of coffee shops, pizza joints, and Mexican restaurants. In a couple more years, all but Pret had been sold again.

It's not like they didn't recognize the problem, they did. First job cuts and first revenue decrease happened under CEO Jack Greenberg in 1998. First quarterly loss of $343 million in 2003 under CEO Jim Cantalupo, a result of the first same store revenue decreases during 2002. They could see that there was a problem, after years of fighting the critics, the lawsuits, the biting documentaries and the anti-globalization attacks.

The trouble for them was adapting fast enough from a standing start. Years of avoiding the conclusions of their critics and the improvements of their competitors had left ingrained habits that afflicted the centre. People in the organization knew there was a problem, but they were unable to gain sufficient attention from the highest, most static, levels. The most imaginative adaptation was happening, as it often does, on the edges.

Experiments by a franchisee in Canada provided the McFlurry but it was in Australia that a culture of willing, almost playful adaptation emerged. The McCafe, the McSalad and the McDouble all emerged because Australia was relatively isolated from the rest of the organization. They were able to experiment, according to their next CEO Charlie Bell, because they felt far enough away from the eyes of senior management to just try whatever creative adaptations seemed to make sense. Bell started working for McDonald's when he was 15, was a store manager by the time he was 19 and understood the nature of the adaptation necessary.

Unfortunately, both McDonald's CEOs responsible for the initial turnaround, Jack and Charlie, died within a couple of years of each other. In 2004, this led to the appointment of Jim Skinner who made one more important contribution to moving from knowing it had to adapt to adapting in a way that worked. He moved from complexity to clarity.

Jim simplified the various strands of strategy into a one-page document entitled the 'Plan to Win' with nine points about making McDonald's the customers' 'favourite place and way to eat'. He insisted on the nine points becoming central to action at every restaurant. He felt that people had to get back to where they would realize what they did was 'not rocket science', but that it was about 'relentless focus on improving' what they had. In his words, this was 'key to the enlightenment of the organization'.

By making it clear what had to happen he made it easier to understand. To encourage people to get involved in making it happen, he reduced the hierarchical barriers between ideas and action. If you hide away the conditions for getting involved you reduce the likelihood of people getting involved. The chances are reduced of finding the constant stream of daily adaptations required to thrive in the existing game, and those necessary to change the nature of the game. Clarity increases engagement.

Humans are an adaptive species. We have succeeded in exploring every climate and settling in almost every extreme our planet can offer. Where we cannot physically cope with the demands of an environment, we equip ourselves with housing, clothing, tools and other forms of technology. We move closer together to increase our chances of survival but also our opportunities for collective learning and action. We have learned to live in cities and create electronic connections between us so that we can share ideas and work together.

Our history is full of individuals and groups seeking to adapt themselves to a situation or the situation to themselves. It is also full of groups who do not adapt their behaviour even though their behaviour is not working. There are plenty of examples of where knowing does not lead to doing. As one US army officer argued:

> The will of the people is now the objective of both General Petraeus and McChrystal's strategy. Yet, it is one thing to dictate requirements about developing host nation relationships and gaining the will of the people, and another to develop [...] leaders adaptive enough to carry out these objectives. [...] The Army does not have the programs in place to develop agile and adaptive leaders needed for this era of persistent conflict.

The officer, Lieutenant Colonel Jeffrey E Pounding, points out that the US army has the necessary knowledge to establish training programmes that would in turn develop the adaptive leaders that would, in turn, establish peace in occupied nations. They recognize the need for more adaptive leaders, they understand the nature of the adaptation but they do not act upon that recognition or that understanding. They fail to adapt.

The result is an unhealthy gap between need and behaviour. And it's a gap that remains unfilled, year after year, month after month, body bag after body bag. It is a chronic failure seemingly unmoved by necessity, death, political pressure, or the repeated attempts of individuals who see the problem and its solution.

Evolution, it has been argued, does not care what we think. It cares about what we do. Evolution selects based on actions. The same can be said even of temporary behavioural adaptation. The success of any particular adaptation is judged by its effectiveness at achieving outcomes in a way that the person, or group, thinks is desirable. It is not enough to think.

Sometimes such training does not take place because adaptive action becomes more effective when failure is discussed. Unfortunately, discussion of failure may not be attractive to leadership obsessed with looking successful in the short term rather than being successful in the long term. There can be an inbuilt defensive mechanism against the development of new adaptations. Overcoming this mechanism is often the key to travelling from one-time recognition to all-the-time adaptability.

Only when the people swarm can they overwhelm the limits of an existing system, for good or bad. Only when they swerve past an obvious objective can they move resources to overwhelming those existing limits.

Rule
16
Get your ambition on

In the past 20 years, Pull & Bear, a Spanish clothing retailer, has opened 704 shops in 48 countries. Over the past year, Gap, the US clothing retailer, has announced the closure of 200 of its 1,426 stores. Pull and Bear claim the 'spirit of youth' as their inspiration; while the success of Gap was based on the youthful rebellion of the 'summer of '69' personified by a master creative, until it grew up, grew old and stopped inspiring anyone.

The way they describe themselves is instructive. Pull & Bear are part of a 'global youth culture', designing spaces and clothes customers love. Gap is an 'iconic retail brand' continuing to build its brand presence around the world. Gap listens to the ghosts of retail past, Pull & Bear follows the voice of potential; the future gives it direction and unlimited energy.

The direction of a human group matters. Limit human aspiration to feeding an idea that is no longer worth the effort and human ability to sustain the system is constrained. It is simpler to engage human interest to create something better than to maintain what already exists. Ambition is how we plug into discretionary creative potential.

Individual ambition may find it difficult to survive in a system limited by the past. After 24 years with the company, Marka

Hansen, president of Gap's North American division, probably thought her work on launching a redesigned logo was certain of success. Or at least support from her colleagues might have been expected. But that's not what happened.

The change from traditional white-on-navy was greeted with aggressive disdain, particularly among tweeters and bloggers. Only a few days later the new logo was abandoned and the online community of khaki-loving brand stalwarts were able to rest easy. Hansen denied, and then confessed her guilt of not making the 'change the right way'. But the real damage was done in the seven years of falling sales before the logo debacle. Customers abandoned Gap long before any threatened redesign.

In 2008, Inditex, the owner of Pull & Bear, became the world's biggest clothing retailer ahead of Gap. Just three years earlier it claimed the top spot in Europe from H&M. By 2011, Inditex had more than 5,000 stores, over 100,000 employees, revenues of nearly $17 billion and profits of more than $2 billion. When Inditex grabbed their crown in 2008, Gap had experienced negative growth in 30 of 38 quarters. Twenty of those negative quarters happened in a row from 2004 onwards. That is the sign of an organization that cannot adapt even when the problem is too big, too obvious to be missed.

Recognition is not sufficient to adapt particularly when that recognition is laced with denial and complacency. The leadership announcement to go with the 2009 results said they were proud to deliver higher earnings per share. The leadership announcement said they were improving their economic model. The leadership model spoke of trajectory of top-line performance and targeted investments. This is not the plain-speaking recognition required to understand and make the necessary adaptations.

Beware the language of confusion. This kind of corporate speak is a clear indication that the culture has lost the ability to see and speak the truth. There is no acknowledgement of the 10 years of poor performance or the 20 years of missed opportunities. Instead of encouraging them to rise to new heights, their competition became they-who-must-not-be-named.

As the Inditex spokesman explained: 'The success of the model is less in being able to adapt what you're offering in the shortest time possible [so that] time is the principal factor to take into account, more so than the costs of production.' Hiding behind excuses and fake success, the people at Gap were unable to learn from the speed of adaptation shown by their chief rival. At this point, they had competed for over 30 years and all they tried to adapt was the logo. It's the culture that needs to change.

Back in 1969, Donald Fisher and his brother Bob decided to open a retail outlet in San Francisco. The story goes that when Donald couldn't find a pair of jeans to fit him, it prompted him to open a store. He picked Levi's because he figured it would always enjoy great margins. His strength was finding undervalued property to provide great retail locations. Merchandising was left to his wife, Doris Fisher, and her team.

This worked until 1976, when Levi's were investigated for price fixing. Margins and stock price crashed. Fisher tried lower-margin Gap-branded clothing which was dissatisfied with scraping along at the bottom of the market. Gap partnered with Ralph Lauren but was unable to manufacture with quality to keep the young fashion star happy. The products were late and the jeans didn't fit well. The partnership didn't last long.

In 1983, Fisher found an answer by hiring Mickey Drexler who had successfully turned around Anne Taylor, a woman's clothing retailer based in New York. Drexler wanted to throw out the low-margin clothes and start again with high quality, high fashion. Fisher fought him but eventually relented. It was to be one of Ron's three claims to fame: starting Gap, hiring Drexler and firing

Drexler. But it was Mickey who transformed the discount-jeans chain into a global megabrand. It was Mickey who redesigned every inch of the stores. It was Mickey who overcame the contradiction between inexpensive and good taste. It was Millard 'Mickey' S Drexler, born 1944 in the Bronx, who brought in stars to make the brand shine. And it was his decisions that helped increase sales from $400 million to $14.5 billion by 2002. The year he was fired.

There were over 100,000 employees who worked at Gap during the Drexler years. Not one of them was selected to lead the company forward after Drexler left. Instead, Paul Pressler was appointed, fresh from 15 years working for the Walt Disney Company. He had run their theme parks, the Disney stores and even the licensing division. Before Disney, Pressler worked for Kenner-Parker who popularized 3.75-inch action figures including the famous range of *Star Wars* toys.

There are lessons to be learned here about individual ambition and ability to adapt. Before he left, Drexler, who knew everything about retail fashion, had made some mistakes. After he joined, Pressler, who knew nothing about retail fashion, would make more mistakes. The difference is that without an understanding of the adaptations that were necessary, it was near impossible for Pressler to learn from his mistakes.

When the next quarter results rose by 12 per cent, polished Pressler was praised. Yet it was too early to give him the credit. The decisions leading to those results were either short-term boosts to sales or came from his predecessor. Products sold today are decided on many months before. The growth was most likely to be successful adaptation by Mickey and his team to the lessons learned from previous disappointments.

Pressler didn't want to work with Drexler's team. Despite their talent having created the clothing that was selling so well, he wanted familiar faces around him. He yearned for people who made him feel comfortable, so he hired ex-Disney colleagues to positions in operations, finance and human resources.

He rejected the corporate motto of 'Own it, do it, get it done' and replaced it with 'Explore, create and exceed together.' Posters were posted. Values were valued. The number of meetings to explain the new culture increased. Meetings stole time from the job of turning around the company. Processes robbed the company of energy, spontaneity and the kind of magical, focused creativity that drives results in a fashion retailer. Instead of looking a year ahead to conjure up the future in time to design it, Gap people were looking at weeks packed full of training and financial reporting. There was no room for the future. The joy had left the building.

It is very tempting to try to remake a new situation to match an old situation. Instead of admitting ignorance, Pressler insisted on doing what he could control. He cut costs by restricting all Gap brands to one supplier of fabric. He cut costs by having all samples made in Asia, not the USA. He did the exact opposite of Inditex. He focused on finance ahead of fashion. He focused on costs instead of growth. He set up blocks to adaptation.

This kind of wrong-headed maladaptation was supported by Gap's owner because Fisher didn't want to admit his error in kicking out Drexler. It was particularly difficult to recognize the mistake because Mickey was already transforming J-Crew from safe national mail-order service to international fashion power-house. The more obvious the mistake the less likely an average leader is to confess. And so adaptation can never be rapid.

Pressler was out by 2007, thanked by Fisher for being a 'great partner' and replaced by Glenn Murphy, ex-CEO of a drug retailer. Drexler had already taken J-Crew into public ownership and turned $609 million in debt into $1 billion revenues. At Gap,

Murphy, who knew nothing about fashion, spent 2008 cutting costs while revenues continued to fall. Inditex had just become the biggest clothes retailer in the world.

'I look at running a store like playing a game. You want to win,' said Don Fisher to an employee question. The problem is that he has restricted his definition of winning to staying in control. It's not impossible. It's not the financial crisis. He has stopped himself from finding a creative successor to Drexler because he is unwilling to adapt to win. Fisher appears to lack the ambition to let the magic back into Gap.

Recent experiments by researchers at the University of Southern California suggest that someone with power may use that power to punish someone who has higher status. They created four groups from 213 volunteers. Each volunteer was randomly assigned to either a high-status or low-status role and asked to work as a partner in a business game. There was a bonus prize of $50 from a draw available for one volunteer.

Volunteers decided what tasks their partner had to do to qualify for the lottery. Both could choose what their partner had to do from a range of 10 tasks, half simple and half demeaning. They could choose to force their partner to complete all tasks or allow their partner to get away with just one task from the list. The difference was that half of the volunteers could decide that they could remove their partner's name from the lottery if they didn't like the tasks they had to complete. As a result they had high power while their partners had low power in the situation.

Those with high status and high power felt it unnecessary to humiliate their partners. Feeling good about themselves, they chose easier and fewer tasks for their co-workers. In complete contrast, those with low status and high power forced their partners through demeaning tasks.

They didn't have to, and they gained nothing monetary through their decision to demean their high-status partner. For most, the power to do something about their feelings of low status was too much to resist. It's important to note that low status was not about power or reward, it was about how the role was perceived by the individual and the group.

Fisher, the owner of the company, often complained about Drexler getting all the credit, praise and attention. As soon as Fisher had the opportunity, he humiliated his rival for status. He hired someone who could manage what existed rather than creating anything to challenge his status as founder. He punished Drexler by not letting him put his mistakes right.

Sometimes, perhaps often, the first people to recognize something, or gain an insight, are not appreciated. The more extreme, or different, or unpleasant, or radical the insight is, the more extreme or unpleasant can be the reaction from those who do not share the view.

Very often those who receive the Nobel Prize have seen something first and have adapted their work to fit what they have seen. On 8 April 1982, Danny Shechtman, a scientist at the Technion-Israel Institute of Technology, saw something that was impossible. As he looked at photos of a rapidly cooled alloy, there were atoms arranged in a pattern that did not repeat itself. They were crystals, yet not crystals. He saw something that should have not existed according to scientific knowledge at the time.

The head of his research group asked him to leave because he was bringing disgrace to them all. It broke so many basic rules that people would not accept that he could be right about what he observed. There was even opposition from Linus Pauling, 'father of molecular biology' and double Noble Prize winner.

Pauling famously rejected the notion saying, 'There is no such thing as quasi-crystals, only quasi-scientists.'

Shechtman persevered. He found one supporter, then a second, then a third. His first paper was rejected, his second accepted but ridiculed by mainstream chemists. He gained increasing belief from mathematicians and physicists outside his direct expertise. At one point, he received a copy of Thomas Kuhn's book on the *Philosophy of Science* and found his experience fighting consensus on its pages.

The quasi-crystal story illustrates the importance of different kinds of adaptability. Pauling could not adapt his position to accept a new discovery in comparison to Shechtman who was unwilling to adapt his position to deny what he had found. Opponents couldn't accept the rewriting of orthodoxy, but eventually adapted to new evidence.

Ambition is not equally distributed, nor is the kind of ambition we have equal in its nature. There are different kinds of ambition. Blind ambition is much criticized, while much endured. Narcissistic ambition can be unattractive to those who deal with the self-obsessed. Low ambitions may keep people in self-limiting situations while ambition to overcome constraints can be an act of imagination that changes the world.

Think back to Bill Gates wanting a computer on every desk. In 1981, this was an ambitious statement. In 1981, this seemed excessive because the personal computer was only just emerging from the hobbyist's workbench and inventor's garage. Ambition is a way of seeing the future. The way we see different futures shapes our actions in the present. We can only change anything in time going forward; ambition is what gets us started.

When Ponoko announces the *world's easiest making system*, they are demonstrating revolutionary ambition. When they shout about the personal factory movement, they have introduced an idea that will not die even if they failed. Ponoko is a clever idea woven together with long-term human trends. We like to build. We like to find products that enhance our lives and solve our problems. Ponoko fulfils both needs.

It's hard to overstate their ambition. They want to make it possible for someone to turn their idea into a real-life product as easy as buying a book on amazon.com. You are invited to upload your idea, buy or modify existing design templates. You can then add your products to an online showroom where they are made to order and delivered to customers.

The production is local or as local as possible. The idea is that people with 3D printers in their homes print the products for delivery to customers. It's like frame knitting in the nineteenth century all over again, with family-sized businesses able to produce customized products to order from their houses, flats and cottages. They imagine a community of ideas made wonderful by increasing involvement and making production easier.

The local factory movement is a world away from the limited ambition of cutting costs to increase earnings. In many ways, 3D printing is characteristic of how technology revolutions happen. It started with curiosity. It continues to be nurtured with a kind of obsessive, altruistic fascination with making new ideas work through adaptation of existing technologies. Ideas are renewed with relentless experimentation.

Woodblock printing goes back nearly 2,000 years where it spread from China to the rest of the world. It took the Chinese, and then the Koreans, another 800 years to figure out movable type. Another 400 years were required for a European to make a printing press. Around 1439, Johannes Gutenberg adapted the movable type idea into something faster, requiring fewer people and costing less money. Many consider his invention as the greatest of the second millennium.

A new typographical age energized the Renaissance throughout Europe. Ideas were able to travel faster between individuals, groups and nations. Opinions and discoveries could be shared. Once shared, the merits of ideas could be debated, critiqued and improved upon. The basis of a more reliable scientific community was made possible by the simple printing press. Scientists could see further by standing on giants' shoulders, and those shoulders were made of books.

Something similar is happening with the internet. Online discussions, critiques and collaborations are much faster than with printed material. Speed may not be everything but if all interactions are of a similar standard then it is almost everything. The more attempts there are at solving something collectively, the more likely a solution is to be found.

Claims are made, objections discussed, and research interests exchanged. There are still benefits to publishing in paper but they may have less to do with making original contributions to human knowledge, much more with perpetuating systems of academic measurement and status.

Those who seek urgent answers and deep understanding will not wait for referreed journals with years of anonymous reviews and revisions. The adaptive process of recognition, understanding and action is accelerated by internet functionality and a collaborative sensibility. Some scientific communities have adapted centuries-old ways of working to the internet.

As a recent example, Ed Nelson, a professor at Princeton, announced that he had found inconsistencies with some of the fundamental principles of mathematics. The principles are known as the Peano axioms and were published in 1889 by Giuseppe Peano, an Italian mathematician.

The Peano axioms are believed by almost all mathematicians to be consistent on the basis of intuition; they seem true. For many, they are considered untouchable tenants of mathematical orthodoxy. So when the claim was made that a proof had been found, significant debate began on the web. Maths bloggers, academics and amateurs, quickly joined in.

Terry Tao, UCLA mathematics prodigy, shared his concerns on his Google+ blog. Those concerns were reported by blogger John Baez, over at the University of Texas. Edward Nelson defended Tao's criticisms about where the error in reasoning was likely to be found. Until after a couple of exchanges, Nelson conceded that his 'original response was wrong' and withdrew his claim. The work leading up to the claim must have taken years. The debunking of the claim leading to its withdrawal took just one day.

The speed is important, as is the manner of the exchange. As soon as an idea is released onto the web, it can be found through search engines by over two billion users. They don't need to be working with the originator of the idea, or to know about the details, they may just stumble upon it. Communities may form around individuals with ideas or the ideas themselves. Terry Tao has over 5,000 people following his discussions online: just a small example of the adaptive power of mass connectivity.

This is the kind of mass experimentation that the personal factory movement imagine. It is also the kind of mass personalization that ambitious visionaries see happening in industries as diverse as medicine, fashion, electronics and toys. They are trying to build systems that can adapt to the imagination, needs and dreams of the global population.

George Church is the kind of man who has ambition beyond the possible, which is exactly what drives him to attempt the impossible. This driven approach to adaptation seeks out necessity. He wants an improved world and so seeks ways of integrating disciplines to create what he wants.

In his lab at Harvard, he surrounds himself with younger people, he says, because 'they will indulge me in my dreams'. He values their inexperience because 'they don't think things are impossible'.

For other more experienced, or less imaginative, people, it is easier to reject ideas as crazy, just because they don't yet work. The chairman of bioethics at Boston University described some of Church's vision as 'in the realm of science fiction' and felt that 'you've got to be foolish to make as much progress as he imagines'. Such thinking doesn't fully recognize the need or opportunity to adapt because it is limited by the current situation.

Thirty years ago, Church was one of the few who recognized the opportunity to sequence the full human genome. His lab was the first to design and build a machine to decode the genome. It cost $3 billion the first time around, so he kept improving it until the price to decode a genome reduced to $5,000. He believes the cost will rapidly lower to less than $250, to become a routine medical test.

He is involved in more than 20 different groups, private and publicly funded, with the aim of bringing together insights from different disciplines and as many resources as he can find. The focus is to map all seven billion of the world's phenotypes, the way we are, with its genotypes, our genetic material. He will start with 100,000 volunteers and each of the 60 million bits that make up their individual genomes.

And that's not all. Next he wants to build machines that will allow individual genomes to be deliberately adapted. They would go beyond genome sequencers to genome adaptors. According to Church, we will build machines to reprogram our individual genomes genetically and epigenetically. The process takes adult stem cells and takes them back to a pluripotent state where they can grow into any cell type.

Our focus here is twofold. First, how easily others reject unorthodox talk as a form of science-fiction-infected irrational exuberance despite the progress that has been made. Perhaps only irrational exuberance can overcome the constraints of previous systems and knowledge? Perhaps only fiction is able to put the limits of the present situation aside for long enough to think our way to a far better place? Ambition takes you further.

Second, this concept of taking back adult cells to a more adaptable state is directly analogous to human systems. Each part of a social group, and each individual in a social group, tends to specialize. This specialization includes economic roles or professions, but it also includes thousands of behaviours that fit into the patterns of behaviour around them. These become habitual, shortcut heuristics, many of which are followed without conscious thought. We may not even know why we are doing something.

Restoring our behaviour to a completely open state is probably not desirable but opening up is essential to allow new adaptation. Getting your ambition on requires a certain letting go of old limitations, forgetting of old constraints, going over the line, and towards new worlds.

Rule
17
Always the beginning

In adaptive terms, if you are still in the game, then it's always the beginning. There are many advantages of adapting first, or adapting best over a long period of time. The winner acquires resources that make them more immune to challenges in the environment. The winner might learn something about winning, and even how best to achieve renewal.

Yet, not winning first, or often, or ever does not stop adapting more successfully in the future. Weaknesses may turn out to be strengths as the situation changes. You can imaginatively rethink your actions so that wherever you are becomes the best place to start.

The features of a winning strategy may become exaggerated over time. Excessive resources may encourage recklessness, waste or complacency. Successful patterns of behaviour can become locked in, so that people mindlessly or unimaginatively repeat actions. They forget how to adapt.

As long as you adapt to survive, there is the possibility of finding a high-level, more effective adaptation. This is particularly true when a group or individual is aware that they are surviving until they find something better. They do not accept survival as a way of living; they have not lowered their expectations to simply cope. Instead, they are waiting in a survival pattern as part of finding a better way; survival is just temporary.

This is not to say that survival is always a choice. Events outside immediate control can combine to ruin the best plan, and move faster than the most rapid adaptation. Accidents, luck, happenstance, serendipity, the unintended consequence and the invisible hand of human actions can overpower individual choice in a number of ways.

In 1991, RitVik was still a fairly small toy distribution company with its headquarters in Ontario, Canada. Its founders, Rita and Victor Bertrand, had wanted to move into some kind of proprietary product that could help them expand worldwide. They noticed the legal and commercial battles that began when the last Lego patent for brick design expired in 1988 and considered how they might take advantage.

With their son, Marc Bertrand, now the CEO of the company, they watched attentively as Tyco, the US toy company, won the right in court to make Lego brick clones and then lost the competitive fight in stores. They concluded that Tyco had failed by competing only on low prices. RitVik was renamed Mega Bloks with its CEO confident the company could adapt the basic Lego template in ways that would allow them to succeed.

It didn't take Lego long to file their first lawsuit, or their second or their third. But they kept losing. Lego's attempts to maintain patent protection through trademark law did not convince courts or regulators. Lego tried to compete with Mega Bloks in the courts rather than in the toyshops. The legal action diverted attention away from the detail of adapting their toys to the behaviour of distributors, adults and children.

Mega Bloks planned on using imaginative variations on the building block idea. They had already launched their very successful oversized brick in 1984. Mothers loved the toddler-friendly design. Lego were slow to respond. After the patents expired, they were able to compete directly in the mini-brick sector for older children and adults. It became an adaptation grand prix with whoever adapted fastest likely to enjoy success.

Mega Bloks did what Lego could not do. It worked with television shows and movies to bring out themed construction sets. There were superhero figures from Marvel comics and the Spider-man trilogy. They created brick sets with Smurfs, Thomas and Friends, Hello Kitty, Lord of the Rings and Harry Potter. It was this constant renewal of the idea of construction bricks that consumers found so attractive and Lego found so daunting.

Between 2003 and 2005, Lego reduced their workforce by 1,000 employees. They reduced the workforce because sales were $500 million lower over the same period. It was part of a turnaround plan that included selling off its theme parks to the same venture capitalist, Blackstone, who had helped fund Mega Bloks' global expansion and flotation on the stock market.

By 2011, Mega Bloks had grown from around 100 people in 1991 to 1,300 employees. Its revenue was nearly $400 million. Lego was still a much bigger company with about $1.75 billion in revenue, but had been provoked into updating its classic bricks and complacent marketing methods. They had successfully copied from the copier.

It was now Lego with the Harry Potter themed franchise. It was now Lego with the Pirates of the Caribbean sets. Lego was able to announce 32 per cent increases in its sales with double-digit growth in more than 130 countries. The adaptation race with Mega Bloks has successfully grown the market for construction bricks far beyond where it was in the comfortable 1990s. After a really tough first decade of denial faced with competition, Lego has spent the second decade transcending the limits of its marketplace. As competitors have joined the adaptation race, they have provoked greater, more imaginative efforts from each other.

Consider Hasbro, who developed their new building block system in 2011 as an extension of their Transformers franchise. Invigorated by the success of three blockbuster movies, and inspired by the licensing success of Megabloks, they combined both ideas with a new line of toys called KRE-O. Each set allows a character from the movie to be built and then transformed into their vehicular form. This would not have happened without Megabloks and increases further the space given to building blocks in superstores in retail centres and online.

The loss of patent protection in 1988 was a new beginning for Lego. Extending their product in 1991 was a new beginning for Mega Bloks. 2011 was a new beginning for Hasbro. Every year, every month, every product was a new beginning regardless of how well, or badly, either had done in the months, decades and days before.

Distractions stop people recognizing the need to adapt. At Lego, disbelief at losing their magical patent protection was followed by belief that they could conjure up legal help from trademark law. These are distractions that move focus from complacency to confusion; both prevent effective adaptation. It is important to choose the best place to focus adaptation efforts, and that place is rarely in law courts since victory here so often delays necessary changes. Shift effort to finding a better equilibrium.

Over at Mega Bloks, there was a legal case relating to the accidental death of a boy who swallowed a toy magnet, followed by a legal challenge to share-dealing among senior management. More problems included a disastrous acquisition, a $459 million loss in 2008, and shares that dropped from $30 to being a penny stock. Organizations that do not renew are likely to stagnate, risking painful existence or even extinction.

Most organizations do not renew themselves more than they think is necessary. Part of this is efficient; they seek to avoid wasting time and resources on change if what they have is already working. There are risks involved in changing direction; it's an update to the human system that may not work, and that will cause problems even if it does work.

Particularly interesting is how the ideas that had made Lego so successful, for instance their founder's motto that 'Only the best is good enough' provided a starting point for their competitor. Mega Bloks moved past some of the constraints that slowed Lego down, providing a new template for success which their bigger competitor eventually emulated and exceeded. Only now is Mega Bloks regrouping with some of the superior adaptations enjoyed by Lego including the links to virtual worlds online.

Finding the right competitor can be a simple way of motivating adaptation. The right competitor increases dissatisfaction with the current situation because they are doing better. They also increase the available options for adaptation because they are trying new approaches.

The combination of the right competitor's actions can provide desire to adapt, belief that adaptation is possible, and the opportunity to do, or exceed, what has already been done. When Apple launched the app store it did more than just provide software to customers, it provided them with competition to the features on the iPhone. Clever, motivated developers looked for gaps; features not provided directly by the operating system. The more significant the gap, the more popular the app. Apple could continue to ignore the gap because the app made it less of a problem for customers. Or build a version of those features into the operating system if that served their purpose.

Yet because it is always the beginning, it is possible for dissatisfaction to never quite provoke action. Unhappiness with the way things are may bubble under the surface, or even be openly discussed. There may never be enough pressure to overcome inertia in the group, until it's too late.

An adaptive social group seeks to renew itself, not because they are forced to by poor results, but because of a deep desire to be better. This perpetual dissatisfaction is driven by an inner need to improve. It's often also linked to an awareness of how the work of the group is perceived. There is recognition of the outside world including customers and competitors, and a desire to adapt what is done internally to succeed.

The CEO of Tata Motors resigned in September 2011. He resigned after just two years, citing 'unavoidable personal circumstances' for his decision but it was still unexpected. The market reacted nervously to the loss of an executive with experience at senior levels of BMW and General Motors. Analysts wondered aloud whether progress would slow or stop.

Within one month, the annual results for Tata were announced. Growth in revenue over the previous 12 months was 42 per cent. Tata now had the cheapest car in the world, the $2,500 Nano, alongside some of the most expensive vehicles. It had adapted its way to compete with the biggest car brands on earth. For many observers, this was just the beginning.

It was all very different in 2008 when, amid global financial panic, Tata Motors bought Jaguar Land Rover (JLR) from Ford for $2.5 billion. Stock holders didn't like the deal and the share price declined 70 per cent over the next 18 months, until they saw the results. From a $308 million loss in the first year, Tata controlled costs and invested time and money until JLR became the fastest-growing luxury car company in the world.

Tata Motors chose to grow by buying other companies. Its leadership team recognized there were benefits and opportunities to rapid growth. They wanted to learn how to improve each company they bought while at the same time learning from each company they bought. By pooling the learning capability of each group the process of acquisition could accelerate their adaptation efforts. They would adapt better together.

Each acquisition, starting with the purchase of Daewoo in 2004, was approached as a learning partnership. This was not about occupation or oppression; instead Tata people were respectful of the talent in each new group whether in Spain, England, Korea, Brazil or Italy. Each purchase was made only if there was some mutual benefit to working as a team.

Tata was not buying new companies to survive, or even to simply exploit them. It was buying into companies to allow it to transcend its origins as a national manufacturer of commercial vehicles under licence. This difference in thinking meant they worked intelligently to achieve the goals it had set before making the purchase.

Thinking their way into a better situation has characterized Tata people since it was started up in 1868 as a trading company by 29-year-old Jamsetji Tata. Within 12 months, he acquired a bankrupt oil mill in Chinchpokli near the Mumbai train line. He adapted it into a cotton mill and sold it profitably. For the rest of his life, he focused on four goals: to start a steel company, a world-class institute, hydro-electric plant and a unique hotel.

One of these was accomplished in 1903 when the mighty Taj Mahal Palace and Tower opened in Mumbai (the same hotel that was attacked by terrorists on 26 November 2008). After his death, his son continued his father's dream by founding Tata Steel, now seventh-largest steel company in the world, and Tata Power, India's oldest and largest energy company.

The next member of the Tata family in charge of the company was French-born, French-speaking and French-raised JRD Tata. Stirred by the aviation exploits of adventurer Louis Blériot, the first man to fly a real plane across the English Channel, the 23-year-old gained his pilot's licence. Within four years he founded India's first commercial airline, which became Air India a couple of years after national independence.

From 1938 when he became chairman of the Tata group, aged 34, to the time he retired 50 years later, the assets of the company increased from around $100 million to more than $5 billion. Just as impressively, he created a working environment that was almost a society within a society, with working conditions that were much better than legally required. He ensured that employees were actively involved in setting the direction of the company. He introduced an eight-hour working day, free medical aid, and accident compensation that started from the time workers left home.

Even more impressively, this growth happened against a background of difficult national conditions. The Licence Raj is the popular name for the centrally planned economic system established in 1947 by Jawaharlal Nehru, India's first post-independence prime minister. Following this system the government issued licences to private businesses based on five-year plans inspired by those of the Soviet Union. India in the 1950s began with high growth, open trade, and hope, but by the 1980s it was plagued by low growth, closed trade, a corrupt licence system and crisis.

It was only in 1991, with only two weeks of dollar reserves left, that India chose to accept liberalization in return for funds from the International Monetary Fund. And in the very same year, Ratan Tata became chairman of the Tata group and produced India's first-ever passenger vehicle. It was criticized, as were subsequent cars, but Tata had the knack of adapting the details of its products to the particular needs of its market.

Tata have cultivated a deep ability to adapt effectively. The current chairman started on the factory floor with other steelworkers, shovelling limestone and caring for the blast furnace. In this way, he gained a valuable understanding of employee life and the work itself.

After working his way up, Ratan was eventually put in charge of a failing electronics division, where he increased market share from 2 per cent to 25 per cent. Next he received the assignment to turn around the oldest part of the company set up by the founder Jamsetji Tata. The chairman of the company denied him the investment needed and so it closed down. These were all demanding situations that ensured he understood the nature of the company and the practical dynamics of trying to improve in a crisis.

He didn't inherit a crisis when he became chairman of the group. Instead he inherited an organization that risked declining if he did not find a way of transcending its limitations. And he inherited the resources to try to help India overcome some of its own economic and social weaknesses.

He made some of the more obvious decisions like reducing the number of businesses, but he also made non-obvious decisions. The international expansion was bold, but the most imaginative was a push towards frugal innovation that could industrialize sustainable answers to the needs of the millions who want what they cannot have.

One of the most famous frugal projects started with an insight. There was recognition that something could change with the dangerous transport used by Indian families. The insight became a series of doodles by a chairman trained in design and bored by long meetings. The doodles became a four-year project worked backwards from the maximum price, $2,500, to design and production techniques that made it possible.

In many ways, it is reminiscent of the origins of the Toyota Prius. An idea from the top inspired by a wider social vision, pushed engineers, partners and material science past existing boundaries. Back in 2008, the Nano had no shortage of books, including mine, praising the concept and the stunning achievement of design over constraints. But this wasn't the end of the story; it was only the beginning. Such is adaptation.

The factory was relocated after attacks from a senior politician. Production was delayed. There were media reports of un-explained fires. The price changed. The target audience found it difficult to afford without credit. The audience who could afford it were put off by its image as a cheap car. The sales network didn't reach people in rural areas.

In one particularly horrendous month, November 2010, they sold just 509 cars from a factory capable of producing 100,000 vehicles a year. The backlash of journalists unhappy at the lack of a fairy-tale ending was severe. It was severe and misguided. The criticism ignores what has been accomplished to produce the world's cheapest car, the value of what has been learned and success so far, and the adaptability prowess of Tata.

In October 2011 the Nano was nominated for the World Design Impact Prize. Throughout the same year, Nano sales grew by 6 per cent compared with only 1 per cent for the overall car market. It has launched an upgrade to the original Nano, and has already dealt with 100,000 orders received since the launch. Competitors are expanding the market.

Ratan made it clear at the start of the project that there would be continual adaptation and improvement of the original car. He is expecting great things of their work with Jaguar Land Rover who can learn from Tata an 'inexpensive way of doing something' while 'Tata learn a better way of doing something'. The company knows it's still a novice, the company knows that its products have failings but it also knows that it is well placed to design cars that better meet the needs of its markets.

When they announced the Indica in December 1998, it was billed as the most modern, first fully Indian passenger car. The complete design and production were handled in-house. It was launched with great fanfare from Tata and withering criticism from car journalists and industry analysts.

Despite the criticism, there were 115,000 orders within a week of the car being available in 1999. In response to complaints about performance, changes were made almost immediately and a second version produced. In less than two years it was the best-selling car in its market segment. A new model arrived in 2008, and in 2011 an all-electric version launched.

This spirit of adaptability is known in India as *jugaad*. It's about improvisation. Jugaad, a Hindi word, is about figuring out a way to make something work even when the correct tool is not available, or there is shortage of resources. That's what the Nano still represents; it's what Tata personifies. They decided to create a 'people's car for India' exactly because it didn't already exist, precisely because it was thought impossible. They have learned that bold steps take them further.

One person's long emergency is another person's long opportunity. While critics scoffed and competitors backed off from the impossible, 500 Tata engineers were busy working to deliver the impossible. They were designing and redesigning. They were getting tired and starting again. But, according to Girish Wagh the chief designer, despite more failures than successes people were motivated to keep trying. Part of this came from the personal involvement of Ratan Tata who removed fear from the process, so that there was only a sense of adventure.

Research indicates that people tire of exactly this kind of repetition. Adaptation fatigue creeps in that stops additional improvement, the effort seems to outweigh the cost of each new idea. If the majority of the social group feel that way, then the situation, product or process becomes fixed. Not because no one can think of a way of making the situation better, but because they are unwilling to pay the emotional price. It's too awful to even consider starting the project again. The end of progress.

Most people are tempted to stick with what they have. The calculation can be made that something better isn't worth the effort, or that the effort will not work. Familiarity leads to passive surrender. Even if what they have is below what they know is possible. Even if what they have is mediocre, disappointing or doomed. The unacceptable is accepted daily.

The ability to start again with enthusiasm is powerful. Knowledge and skill are valuable yet a key feature of adaptation effectiveness is the willingness of people to relentlessly, even joyously, throw themselves back into the never-ending work of perfect ideas and better futures.

Final words

When people can't grow, economies can't grow. More importantly, when people can't grow, societies can't grow. The seemingly endless creativity invested into deadly or oppressive cat-and-mouse games would be better spent on unravelling the game. We may swerve past the unhappy plateaus to more glorious social harmony or swarm past shallow expectations to replace them with a sense of deep fulfilling progress.

This book is about adaptation beyond survival. To survive is necessary but to only survive is unsatisfactory. Social groups must continue to exist if they want the opportunity to adapt but continued existence does not ensure happy adaptation.

We've examined three steps to deliberate adaptation. The steps interact with unintended consequences and unplanned events but they still start out with the deliberate intention to adapt the situation in a desirable way.

The first step is to recognize the need for adaptation. It may start with something as simple as knowing something is wrong, fearing that something will go wrong, or wanting something to be better. Quite often, a lone voice, or minority, recognizes that need. A majority may even want some part of a situation to be improved; it is less common for everyone to agree on the nature of the improvement required.

Some recognize patterns that can be changed years, even centuries, before survival is threatened. They may even recognize opportunity for transcending limits that will bring them, and their immediate social group, little benefit. These people are sensitive to events before their birth and after their death, they see further and care about what will happen beyond their own temporary existence.

Others recognize the need for adaptation when it is too late for survival or only find significant actions that bring them advantage in the moment that they act, or fairly soon afterwards. For those reading who find satisfaction in contributing to life beyond the moment, it is your responsibility to consider how to take action towards that better world.

The second step is to understand the required adaptation. Many more people recognize the vague need to change than understand the precise changes required.

Adaptation is about how well behaviour fits to a particular circumstance, and this includes the ability to adapt the circumstance. It is not about whether one social group is better or smarter or kinder or stronger than a competing group. Evolution is not about fitness but fit.

Similarly, a social group may establish an equilibrium that is completely unsatisfactory, even doomed to eventual collapse, simply because that pattern of behaviour is the way the group interrelates. Not because it's good for the group, not because the group wants it this way, and not because the individuals are satisfied with the equilibrium.

Many in the group may recognize the problems. All may be dissatisfied with the mechanics of the situation. But recognition and dissatisfaction are not sufficient to lead to any improvement. Dissatisfied individuals may lack the imagination to see an alternative, or the expertise to design one, or the influence to alter the way the group behaves. A social group may stumble its way to a situation without very much deliberate effort to determine the shape of that situation. Survival, or even success, may simply be the combination of individual interactions over time, where the complexity is not intended as part of a grand plan, but the accumulation of actions.

Imagination separates unthinking repetition from adaptive iteration. Learning to adapt more successfully is the art of winning. And it is particularly valuable to become better at adaptation during times of significant uncertainty; more so when the nature of these uncertain times is undesirable to the majority of our planet's seven billion people.

Just as we have in the past, we can find new ways of working together to allow us to renew our social groups and structures. Nothing here is fixed, so very little has to be accepted as final in the ways that we interrelate and collaborate. Adaptability is the key human trait and it can only be used via unconstrained imagination.

The third step is to make the required adaptation. Recognizing the need to adapt is a good start; understanding the precise changes necessary is important, yet if there is no change there will be a bad ending.

Change is inevitable but progress is not. It is strange to how often attempts are made to change without any change being made. We understand, or some of us understand, that a particular transformation is vital, urgent, important, and desirable but somehow it is avoided. Too often there are changes made, perhaps hugely disruptive, expensive changes without moving forward. No better place is reached; no better game is played, so much so that the time and energy expended can appear worse than doing nothing.

Social groups create their own rules but they are also governed, or at least influenced, by the rules they have made. This means that rules made in the past set the context for discussions about what to do now and what to do in the future. Traditions based on what people experienced decades or centuries ago can influence the way you look at a problem, or the way that other people see a situation. As a result, people make decisions based on the ways things were without ever really adapting to the way things are or could be.

Most social groups have a strong collective bias towards keeping things the way they are even when individually they would like to see change. A mixture of what is said, and what is not said, manages to avoid discussing the really tricky issues. And when difficult issues are discussed they will not necessarily lead to coherent transformation in the longer term. It's a form of social homeostasis, or defensive routine that tries to put things back the way they were over and over again, even if those ways are impossible or counterproductive.

Your deliberate efforts to provoke adaptation that leads to a winning position should focus on the smallest possible change to create the biggest possible long-term impact. Each of the examples explored in this book have revealed how relatively small parts of a social system were altered so that the system itself was then altered. Once a better system is established, the various parts of that system will naturally compete to keep it that way. You have transcended the original situation when it would take more effort to go back than to stay in your new healthier, happier place. Understanding how to transcend is the essence of human progress. There really has never been a more important skill than understanding the art of winning amid uncertainty.

Acknowledgements

This book has origins and because it may be read by some of the people who influenced its writing, it seems prudent to mention them. For instance, there's my mother who taught me the value of books, science, curiosity and still acts as unofficial researcher handing me newspaper clippings and journal articles. And there's my father who introduced me to various thought-provoking authors and prompted the desire to write.

It would be smart of me to acknowledge the vital and remarkable stream of ideas available to me on the information-sharing service Twitter. Its value in sharing and refining ideas is hard to overestimate. It is the tool of the great renewal, perfectly timed to allow us to adapt our way out of our great, global upheaval. It's not about celebrities; it's about sharing hopes, thoughts, knowledge and common desire for something better.

References

Rule 1 Play your own game

1   Harlan K. Ullman and James P. Wade, *Shock And Awe: Achieving Rapid Dominance* (National Defense University, 1996), XXIV.
2   Blakesley, Paul J. 'Shock and Awe: A Widely Misunderstood Effect'. *United States Army Command and General Staff College*, 17 June 2004.
3   'A Brief, Bitter War for Iraq's Military Officers; Self-Deception a Factor in Defeat', William Branigin; *The Washington Post*; 27 April 2003.
4   'In the chaos of Iraq, one project is on target: a giant US embassy', Daniel McGrory, *The Times*, 3 May 2006.
5   Various: http://en.wikipedia.org/wiki/Casualties_of_the_Iraq_War
6   Tim Harford, *Adapt: Why Success Always Starts with Failure* (New Yor: Farrar, Strauss and Giroux, 2011).
7   'Pfizer's Future: A Niche Blockbuster', Jonathan D. Rockoff, *The Wall Street Journal*, 30 August 2011

Rule 2 All failure is failure to adapt

1   'Ford refuses bailout despite $14.6 billion loss', Times Online, Christine Seib, 29 January 2009.
2   An interview with Ford CEO Alan Mulally, Molly Wood, CNET, CES 2010. Available at: http://video.answers.com/an-interview-with-ford-ceo-alan-mulally-259735403
3   'Ford bailout money unnecessary, company says', Huffington Post, Kimberly S. Johnson and Tom Krisher, 10 December 2008. Available at: http://www.huffingtonpost.com/2008/12/10/ford-bailout-money-unnece_n_149824.html

4 'Why the Ford-Toyota hybrid tie-up is a big deal', Martin
   LaMonica, 22 August 2011, Green Tech, news.cnet.com.
   Available at: http://news.cnet.com/8301-11128_3-20095547-54/
   why-the-ford-toyota-hybrid-tie-up-is-a-big-deal/

Rule 3 Embrace unacceptable wisdom

1 'Italian town Filettino declares independence', BBC News,
   David Willey, 3 September 2011.
2 'America's Favourite Jeans Go Waterless', Brittany Redden,
   Cliché Magazine, 11 August 2011. Available at:
   http://www.clichemag.com/2011/08/11/americas-favorite-jeans-
   go-water-less/
3 'Levi's Water<Less Launch', 8 November 2010, Contagious.com
4 *Rebels in Groups: Dissent, Deviance, Difference and Defiance*,
   2011, Edited by Joland Jetten and Matthew J. Hornsey, Wiley-
   Blackwell.
5 'Levi's Water<Less Jeans, Will Save Over 16 Million Gallons
   of H2O by Spring 2011', Ariel Schwartz, *Fast Company*,
   3 November 2010.
6 *Obedience to Authority: An Experimental View*, 1974, Stanley
   Milgram, Harper Collins.
7 'Resisting Authority: A Personal Account of the Milgram
   Obedience Experiments', Joseph Dimow, *Jewish Currents*,
   January 2004. Available at: http://www.jewishcurrents.org/
   2004-jan-dimow.htm
8 'Could a Form of Ecstasy Fight Cancer?' Maia Szalavitz, *Time
   Magazine*, 23 August 2011. Available at: http://healthland.time.com/
   2011/08/23/could-a-form-of-ecstasy-fight-cancer/
9 '5 Years After: Portugal's Drug Decriminalization Policy Shows
   Positive Results', Brian Vastag, *Scientific American*, 7 April 2009.
10 'What Britain could learn from Portugal's drug policy',
   Peter Beaumont, *The Observer*, 5 September 2010.
11 'Decriminalising Drugs a Success, says Report', Maia Szalavitz,
   Time Magazine, 26 April 2009.
12 *Drug Decriminalization in Portugal, Lessons for Creating Fair and
   Successful Drug Policies*, Glenn Greenwald, Cato Institute, 2009.

13 'Mexico's Drug War: Can President Calderon Win?'Daniel Tovrov, *International Business Times*, 5 September 2011.

14 'AP IMPACT: After 40 years, $1 trillion, US War on Drugs has failed to meet any of it's goals', Fox News, 13 May 2010, Associated Press. Available at: http://www.foxnews.com/world/2010/05/13/ap-impact-years-trillion-war-drugs-failed-meet-goals/

Rule 4 F*** with the rules

1 'Traits Underlying the Capacity of Ant Colonies to Adapt to Disturbance and Stress Regimes', Timothy A. Linksvayer and Marco A. Janssen, 2008, *Systems Research and Behavioral Science*.

2 'GQ&A: Christian Horner', Delphine Chui, *GQ Magazine*, 12 July 2011. Available at: http://www.gq-magazine.co.uk/entertainment/articles/2011-07/12/gq-sport-christian-horner-red-bull-racing-team-principal-interview

3 'A New Formula', Dominic Bliss, *GQ Magazine*, 16 May 2011.

4 'The Wings Behind Red Bull', Holly McCluskey, *The Sun*, 16 June 2011.

5 'Bernie Ecclestone hits back at Ferrari head by exposing the teams "special deal"', Edward Gorman, *The Times*, 20 December 2008.

6 'F16 pilot was ready to give her life on Sept. 11', Steve Hendrix, *Washington Post*, 9 September 2011.

Rule 5 Stability is a dangerous illusion

1 'UBS needs to restore trust, profitability and stability says Rohner', Clive Horwood, euromoney.com, February 2009.

2 J. Eisert, M. Wilkens and M. Lewenstein, 1999, 'Quantum Games and Quantum Strategies', *Physical Review Letters*, 83, 3077.

3 'Everyone wins in quantum games', Philip Ball, 18 October 1999, Available at: http://www.nature.com/news/1998/991021/full/news991021-3.html

4 'How Israel Wages Game Theory Warfare', Jeff Gates, 20 August 2009. Available at: http://www.intifada-palestine.com/2009/08/how-israel-wages-game-theory-warfare/

5 'Experimental Realization of Quantum Games on a Quantum Computer', Jiangfeng Du, Hui Li, Xiaodong Xu, Mingjun Shi, Jihui Wu, Xianyi Zhou and Rongdian Han, 2002, *Physical Review Letters*, 88, 137902, American Physical Society.

6 'An invitation to Quantum Game Theory', 2002, Edward W. Piotrowski and Jan Sladkowski, *International Journal of Theoretical Physics*, Volume 42, Number 5, 1089–99.

7 'Transitivity of an Entangled Choice', 2011, Marcin Makowski and Edward W. Piotrowski, *Journal of Physics A: Mathematical and Theoretical*, Volume 33, Number 7.

8 Ian Schreiber, 'Game Balance Concepts', 2010. Available at: http://gamebalanceconcepts.wordpress.com/2010/09/01/level-9-intransitive-mechanics/

9 Thomas C. Schelling, *The Strategy of Conflict*, 1999, Harvard University Press. (Originally published in 1960.)

10 'A Curious Case of Exceptionalism: Non-partitionist approaches to ethnic conflict regulation and the question of Palestine', Ali Abunimah, Ethnopolitics, Volume 10, Issue 3–4, 2011.

11 'The Strategy of Manipulating Conflict', 2011, Sandeep Baliga and Tomas Sjostrom, under review for the *American Economic Review*, draft published on the Kellogg School of Management Website.

12 *Cost of Conflict in the Middle East*, 2011, Strategic Foresight Group.

13 *Joint Israeli Palestinian Poll, November–December 2010*, The Harry S. Truman Institute for the Advancement of Peace.

14 Robert Axelrod and William D. Hamilton (27 March 1981), 'The Evolution of Cooperation', *Science*, 211: 1390–96.

15 Robert Axelrod (1984, 2006), *The Evolution of Cooperation*, Basic Books.

16 Robert Axelrod (1997), *The Complexity of Cooperation*, Princeton University Press.

17 Karl Sigmund, Ernest Fehr and Martin A. Nowak(January 2002), 'The Economics of Fair Play', *Scientific American*: 82–87.

18 Robert L. Trivers(March 1971), 'The Evolution of Reciprocal Altruism', *Quarterly Review of Biology*, 46: 35–57.

19 Gretchen Vogel (20 February 2004), News Focus: The Evolution of the Golden Rule, *Science*, 303 (5661): 1128–31.

20 Anton David Lowenberg and William H. Kaempfer, *The Origins and Demise of South African Apartheid: A Public Choice Analysis*, University of Michigan.

21 'South Africa: Adapt or Die', 15 October 1979, *Time Magazine*.

22 'Strange Bedfellows: Mandela, de Klerk, and the New South Africa', Mark Gevisser, *Foreign Affairs*, January/February 2000.

23 'The Strategy of Manipulating Conflict', 2011, Sandeep Baliga, Working Paper, Kellogg School of Management.

24 David A. Meyer, 'Quantum strategies', *Physical Review Letters*, 82, 1052–55 (1999).

25 Jens Eisert, Martin Wilkens and Maciej Lewenstein, 'Quantum Games and Quantum Strategies', *Physical Review Letters*, 83, 3077–80 (1999).

Rule 6 Stupid survives until smart succeeds

1 'Can You See With Your Tongue', Michael Abrams, *Discover Magazine*, June 2003.

2 'Late postacute neurologic rehabilitation: neuroscience, engineering, and clinical programs', Paul Bach-y-Rita, *Archives of Physical Medicine and Rehabilitation*, Volume 84, Issue 8, August 2003, 1100–08.

3 'Theoretical basis for brain elasticity after a TBI', Paul Bach-y-Rita, 2003, *Brain Injury*, Volume 17, Number 8, 643–51.

4 Norman Doidge, *The Brain That Changes Itself*, 2008, Penguin.

5 Thomas Kuhn, *The Structure of Scientific Revolutions*, 1962, University of Chicago Press.

6 'Borders Books, A Victim of the Decline in Hardcover Books, Shift to E-books and State of the Book Retail Industry', PBT Consulting, 19 July 2011. Available at:

http://tommytoy.typepad.com/tommy-toy-pbt-consultin/ 2011/07/
borders-group-inc-said-it-would-liquidate-after-the-second-largest-
us-bookstore-chain-failed-to-receive-any-offers-to-sa.html

7 'Is there hope for small bookstores in a digital age?' Bob
Minzesheimer, *US Today*, 10 February 2010. Available at:
http://www.usatoday.com/life/books/news/
2011-02-10-1Abookstores10_CV_N.htm

8 'Will Barnes & Noble win the book wars?' Michael Brush,
MSN Money Insight, 16 April 2008. Available at:
http://articles.moneycentral.msn.com/Investing/CompanyFocus/
WillBarnesAndNobleWinTheBookWars.aspx

9 'Border's CEO resigns', 21 April 1999, CNN.com. Available at:
http://money.cnn.com/1999/04/21/companies/borders/

10 'Timeline: From the founding of Borders in Ann Arbor to
Chapter 11 bankruptcy', 16 February 2011, Nathan Bomey,
AnneArbor.com. Available at: http://www.annarbor.com/
business-review/timeline-of-borders-groups-decline/

11 Robert Spector, *Amazon.com: Get Big Fast*, 2002, Harper
Paperbacks.

12 S. Kalpanic, *Inside the Giant Machine, An Amazon.com Story*,
2011, CreateSpace.

13 Richard L. Brandt, *One Click: Jeff Bezos and the Rise of
Amazon.com*, 2011, Portfolio Hardcover.

14 'Border's Fall From Grace', *Publishers Weekly*, Jim Milliot,
21 February 2011. Available at: http://www.publishersweekly.com/
pw/by-topic/industry-news/bookselling/article/46223-borders-s-
fall-from-grace.html

15 'Strategy as vector and the inertia of co-evolutionary lock-in',
2002, Robert A. Burgelman, Research Paper No. 1745, Stanford
Graduate School of Business.

Rule 7 Learning fast better than failing fast

1 'Tropicana Line's Sales Plunge 20% Post-Rebranding, OJ Rivals
Posted Double Digit Increases as Pure Premium Plummeted',
Natalie Zmuda, *Advertising Age*, 2 April 2009. Available at:

http://adage.com/article/news/tropicana-line-s-sales-plunge-20-post-rebranding/135735/

2 'Why did BMW buy Rover?', Leslie Button. Available at: http://www.aronline.co.uk/index.htm?whydbbrf.htm

3 Vannevar Bush (1970), *Pieces of the Action*, New York: William Morrow and Company, Inc.

4 Adam Lashinsky, Sr., 'How Apple works: Inside the world's biggest startup', *Fortune*, 9 May 2011.

Rule 8   Plan B matters most

1 'Tackling Unconscious Bias in Hiring Practices: The Plight of the Rooney Rule', Brian W. Collins, 2007, *NYU Law Review*, Volume 82, Number 3.

2 'NFL gets high marks for racial diversity', Associated Press, 15 September 2011, ESPN.

3 Jared Diamond, *Collapse: How societies choose to succeed or fail*, 2005, Penguin Books.

4 Terry Hunt and Carl Lipo, *The Statues That Walked: The Unravelling of the Mystery of Easter Island*, 2011, New York: Free Press.

5 'Easter Island looks to the future', Jayne Clark, *USA Today*, 4 January 2007.

6 'Time Warner Should Read Hasting's Lips', Martin Peers, WSJ Digital Edition, 20 September 2011. Available at: http://online.wsj.com/article/SB1000142405311190419460457 6580952954105990.html

Rule 9 Free radicals

1 David Kirkpatrick, *The Facebook Effect*, (2010), Virgin Books.

2 Niall Harbison, 'Change The Music Industry Forever Today', *Simply Zesty*, 22 September 2011.

3 Russell Ackoff, 'The Art and Science of Mess Management', *The Institute of Management Sciences*, Volume 11, Number 1, February 1981.

4 'Sean Parker: Agent of Disruption', Steven Bertoni, *Forbes Magazine*, 21 September 2011.

5 'Saying Yes to Mess', Penelope Green, *New York Times*, 21 December 2006.

6 'Opportunity Recognition as Pattern Recognition: How Entrepreneurs "Connect the Dots" to Identify New Business Opportunities', Robert A. Baron, February 2006, Academy of Management Perspectives.

7 Larry E. Greiner, 'Evolution and Revolution as Organizations Grow', *Family Business Review*, Volume 10, Number 4, December 1997.

8 Anne Sigismund Huff, James Oran Huff and Pamela S. Barr, *When Firms Change Direction*, 2000, Oxford University Press.

9 Peter Hedstrom, *Dissecting the Social*, 2005, Cambridge University Press.

10 Howard Schultz and Joanne Gordon, *Onward: How Starbucks Fought For Its Life Without Losing Its Soul*, 2011, Rodale Books.

11 'The First Clone', Joannie Fischer, 25 November 2001, *US News*, Money & Business.

12 Bob Berman and Robert Lanza, *Biocentrism*, 2010, BenBella Books.

13 Anthony Atala, Robert Lanza, James A. Thomson and Robert Nerem, *Principles of Regenerative Medicine*, 2010, Academic Press.

14 'Fight for the Right to Clone', Pamela Weintraub, *Discover Magazine*, 19 August 2008.

15 'Starbucks Chief Executive Orin Smith Announces Upcoming Retirement; North America President Jim Donald Promoted to CEO Designate', *Business Wire*, 12 October 2004.

16 Orin C. Smith, 'Managing Growth and Leadership Change at Starbucks', *Ethix Magazine*, 1 April 2005, Center for Integrity in Business, Seattle Pacific University.

17 'Liam Hudson, Iconoclastic Research In Psychology, Obituaries', Robert T. Dean, *The Independent*, 30 May 2005.

18 Liam Hudson, *Contrary Imaginations: A Psychological Study of the English Schoolboy*, 1966, Methuen. (Reprinted in 1967, 1972, 1974).

19 'Advantage of Foreignness in Innovation', 2011, *Strategic Management Journal*, C. Annique Un, Wiley, Volume 32, 1232–42.

Rule 10 Think better together

1 'Leymah Gbowee: Peace Warrior for Liberia', Ode: The Online Community for Intelligent Optimists, Peacecorso. Available at: http://www.odemagazine.com/blogs/readers_blog/9001/leymah_gbowee_peace_warrior_for_liberia

2 'Profile: Leymah Gbowee, Liberia's Peace Warrior', BBC News, 7 October 2011. Available at: http://www.bbc.co.uk/news/world-africa-15215312

3 'Anonymous Letter Bemoans RIM management woes', Erica Ogg, 30 June 2011. Available at: CNET.com, http://news.cnet.com/8301-31021_3-20075817-260/anonymous-letter-bemoans-rim-management-woes/

4 'RIM Faces Hard Questions at this Week's Developers Conference', Ian Paul, PCWorld.com, 17 October 2011. Available at: http://www.pcworld.com/article/242019/rim_faces_hard_questions_at_this_weeks_developers_conference.html

5 'RIM's Free-App Peace Offering Gets Booed', Jennifer Booton, 17 October 2011. Available at: http://www.foxbusiness.com/industries/ 2011/10/17/rim-to-offer-apps-to-disgruntled-blackberry-customers/

6 'BlackBerry outage removes differences between managers, workers', Rahul Roushan, DNA, 15 October 2011. Available at: http://www.dnaindia.com/analysis/report_blackberry-outage-removes-difference-between-managers-workers_1598932

7 'RIM Enters Crisis Management Mode ... But Is It Too Late', Tom Loftus, 13 October 2011, *Wall Street Journal*. Available at: http://blogs.wsj.com/digits/2011/10/13/rim-enters-crisis-management-mode-but-is-it-too-late/

8 'RIM: iPhone is no threat to Blackberry', Times Online, 5 March 2007.

9 'RIM misses on revenue, announces layoffs', Erica Ogg, 16 June 2011, CNET.com. Available at: http://news.cnet.com/8301-31021_3-20071715-260/rim-misses-on-revenue-announces-layoffs/

10 'Did RIM's arrogance screw up the BlackBerry Playbook?' Brightsideofthenews.com 21 April 2011, John Oram. Available at: http://www.brightsideofnews.com/news/2011/4/21/did-rims-arrogance-screwed-up-blackberry-playbook.aspx

11 'All the Dumb Things RIM's CEOs Said While Apple and Android Ate Their Lunch', Jay Yarow, 16 September 2011, Business Insider. Available at: http://www.businessinsider.com/rim-ceo-quotes-2011-9

12 'RIM Employees Pen Letters Agreeing with Anonymous Exec', Adam Mills, 1 July 2011, Gotta Be Mobile. Available at: http://www.gottabemobile.com/2011/07/01/rim-employees-pen-letters-agreeing-with-anonymous-exec/

13 James Howard Kunstler, *The Long Emergency: Surviving the Converging Catastrophes of the Twenty-First Century*, 2005, Grove-Atlantic.

14 'What You Don't Know About M-Pesa', Olga Morawczynski, 14 July 2009, CGAP. Available at: http://technology.cgap.org/2009/07/14/what-you-dont-know-about-m-pesa/

15 AJ A. Bostian, Charles A. Holt, Sanjay Jain and Kamalini Ramdas, 'Adaptive Learning and Forward Thinking in the Newsvendor Game with Transshipments: An Experiment with Undergraduate and MBA Students', *Bostonian*, 12 November 2010.

16 Philip Munz, Ioan Hudea, Joe Imad and Robert J. Smith, 'When Zombies Attack!: Mathematical Modelling of an Outbreak of Zombie Infection', [pdf] In J.M. Tchuenche and C. Chiyaka (eds) *Infectious Disease Modelling Research Progress*, 2009, Nova Science Publishers Inc., pp. 133–50.

17 'Book Review of *Adaptive Thinking: Rationality in the Real World*. By Gerd Gigerenzer. Oxford, Oxford University Press, 2000', in *Evolutionary Psychology*, 2003. 1: 172–87, by Earl Hunt, Professor (Emeritus) of Psychology, Department of Psychology, University of Washington, Seattle.

18 'What You Don't Know About M-Pesa', Olga Morawczynski, 14 July 2009, CGAP.

19 'Designing Mobile Money Services: Lessons From M-Pesa', Olga Morawczynski, *Ignacio Mas*, Spring 2009, Vol. 4, No. 2, 77–91.

Rule 11 Get a kick-ass partner

1 'Call of Duty XP Panel: Zombies!' Gamespot.com, 3 September 2011. Available at: http://au.gamespot.com/shows/on-the-spot/?event=cod_xp_panel_zombies20110903

2 'NaziZombies, Ray Guns and Magic Chests', Haxington Post, 11 November 2008. Available at: http://www.jessesnyder.org/trenches/?p=42

3 'Could Spiderman the Musical be the Biggest Flop in Broadway History?' *The Week*, 12 January 2011.

4 'Broadway Bombshell', Michael Riedel, *New York Post*, 30 May 2010.

5 'Spider 2.0: Is it Fixed? Spider-Man Turn Off The Dark Review', Jonathan Mandell, 13 June 2011. Available at: http://www.thefastertimes.com/newyorktheater/ 2011/06/13/spider-man-turn-off-the-dark-review/

6 'The Legend of Julie Taymor: Fringe Musical Mocks Director and Spiderman', Mark Kennedy, *Huffington Post*, 17 August 2011.

Rule 12 Never grow up

1 'HP's One Year Plan', Al Lewis, Wall Street Journal Online, 28 August 2011. Available at: http://online.wsj.com/article/SB10001424053111904787404576535211589514334.htm

2 'Computers take charge by studying patterns', Mike Lynch, *Financial Times*, 16 June 2010. Available at: http://www.ft.com/cms/s/0/b395fe8a-774d-11df-ba79-00144feabdc0.html#axzz1X8DWxpSV

3 'Leo Apotheker's HP never wanted webOS to succeed', Steven J. Vaughan-Nichols, *Between The Lines*, 19 August 2011. Available at: http://www.zdnet.com/blog/btl/leo-apothekers-hp-never-wanted-webos-to-succeed/55543

4 'Pranks at Microsoft', Hans Spiller, Nov–Dec 1996. Available at: http://www.exmsft.com/~hanss/pranks.htm

5 'How Chinese Street Ballers Inspired Nike's HyperFuse Tech', John Pavlus, *Fastcodesign*, 29 July 2011.

Rule 13 Hierarchy is fossil fuel

1 See: http://online.wsj.com/article/SB1000142405311190471660 4576544740553600386.html?google_editors_picks=true

2 'Playstation 3 "hacked" by iPhone cracker', Jonathan Fildes, BBC News online, 25 January 2010. Available at: http://news.bbc.co.uk/1/hi/8478764.stm

3 'George Hotz: I got sued for "making Sony mad"', David Hinkle, Joystiq, 14 January 2011. Available at: http://www.joystiq.com/2011/01/14/george-hotz-i-got-sued-for-making-sony-mad/#continued

4 'Geohot raps to Sony's Playstation 3 Lawsuit', Rajesh Pandey, Techie Buzz, 13 February 2011. Available at: http://techie-buzz.com/tech-news/geohot-raps-to-sony-ps3-lawsuit.html

5 'Sony: 3 million more Playstation members since attacks', Hayley Tsukayama, 2 September 2011. Available at: http://www.washingtonpost.com/business/economy/sony-3-million-more-playstation-members-since-attacks/ 2011/09/02/gIQAEH1OxJ_story.html

6 'George Hotz comments on the PSN debacle', Mike Luttrell, *TG Daily*, 28 April 2011. Available at: http://www.tgdaily.com/games-and-entertainment-brief/55631-george-hotz-comments-on-the-psn-debacle

Rule 14 Keep the ball

1 'Billy Beane's Failures Have Set The Oakland A's Behind After A Promising 2006', Juan Sarinas, *Bleacher Report*, 24 March 2010.

2 'How Does Oregon Football Keep Winning', Michael Kruse, *Grantland*, 30 August 2011. Available at: http://www.grantland.com/story/_/id/6909937/how-does-oregon-football-keep-winning

3 '1970s Month: The Oranje Revolution', *The Equaliser*, 12 May 2011. Available at: http://equaliserfootball.com/2011/05/12/oranje-revolution/

4 'World Cup 2010 Final: Andrés Iniesta finds key for Spain to beat Holland, Kevin McCarra at Soccer City', guardian.co.uk, 11 July 2010.

5 'In An About-Face, Under Armour Will Introduce Cotton Apparel', Monte Burke, *Forbes*, 26 January 2011. Available at: http://www.forbes.com/sites/monteburke/ 2011/01/26/in-an-about-face-under-armour-will-introduce-cotton-apparel/

Rule 15 Swerve and swarm

1 'Snitching for pay. Available at: http://www.nytimes.com/
2011/09/29/world/asia/in-south-korea-where-digital-tattling-is-a-
growth-industry.html

2 Ake E Andersson, 'Creative People Need Creative Cities', in David
Emanuel Andersson, Ake E. Andersson and Charlotta Mellander,
Handbook of Creative Cities, Edward Elgar Publishing, 2011.

3 'Cognitive Systems and the Supersized Mind'. Available at:
http://hci.ucsd.edu/102a/readings/SSMSymp/Rupert.pdf

4 'Changing Army Culture: Creative Adaptive and Critical
Thinking Officer Corps', Colonel Frederick S. Clarke, Strategy
Research Project, USAWC Class of 2008. Available at:
http://www.dtic.mil/cgi-bin/GetTRDoc?Location=U2&doc=GetT
RDoc.pdf&AD=ADA478309

5 'Capturing the High Ground: Army Adaptive Leadership during
an Era of Persistent Conflict', Lieutenant Colonel Jeffrey E.
Pounding, United States Army National Guard, USAWC Class of
2010. Available at: http://www.dtic.mil/cgi-bin/GetTRDoc?AD=
ADA544368&Location=U2&doc=GetTRDoc.pdf

6 David Cole, 'The Chinese Room Argument', *The Stanford
Encyclopedia of Philosophy* (Winter 2009 Edition), Edward N.
Zalta (ed.). Available at: http://plato.stanford.edu/archives/
win2009/entries/chinese-room/

7 'The Hot Hand in Basketball: Fallacy or Adaptive Thinking?'
Bruce D. Burns, Department of Psychology, Michigan State
University, 2003/2004.

8 '4G Glasses', Jim Frederick, *Time Magazine*, 25 November 2002.

9 'Hong Kong's Poorest Living in Coffin Homes', Benjamin
Gottlieb and Kristie Hang, 26 July 2011, cnn.com

10 'Hong Kong's Pre-Eminent Social Housing Pioneer Honoured in
the UK', 28 June 2011, www.dur.ac.uk

11 'Penthouse Slums: The Rooftop Shanty Towns of Hong Kong'.
Available at: http://dornob.com/penthouse-slums-the-rooftop-
shanty-towns-of-hong-kong/

12 'Shek Kip Mei Estate: Taste 60s and 70s in Old Housing',
Shermaine Ho. Available at: http://www.com.cuhk.edu.hk/
varsity/0505/our_community2.htm

13 'Poverty blights the dream of Hong Kong', David Pilling, *The Financial Times*, 17 March 2010. Available at: http://www.ft.com/cms/s/0/f7f9bdfc-3204-11df-a8d1-00144feabdc0.html#axzz1butrOu3Y

14 'Occupy Wall Street: Adbusters Organization that Started The Movement Inspired by Anna Hazare', Rajiv Banerjee, *The Economic Times*, 26 October 2011. Available at: http://articles.economictimes.indiatimes.com/2011-10-26/news/30324122_1_tv-station-anna-hazare-jamming

15 '#OccupyWallStreet, A Shift in Revolutionary Tactics', Adbusters Blog, 13 July 2011. Available at: http://www.adbusters.org/blogs/adbusters-blog/occupywallstreet.html

16 'The Whole World Is Watching: Occupy Wall Street Stares Down the NYPD', Ishaan Tharoor and Nate Rawlings, 14 October 2011. Available at: http://www.time.com/time/nation/article/0,8599,2096976,00.html

17 'St Paul's Cathedral Protests: Infamous Flash Mobs', *The Telegraph*, 26 October 2011. Available at: http://www.telegraph.co.uk/news/religion/8850441/St-Pauls-Cathedral-protests-infamous-flashmobs.html

18 'How Jim Skinner, McDonald's Beat the Recession', Peter Romeo, *QSR Magazine*, May 2010.

19 'Australian Chief Breaks Tradition at McDonalds', Stephen Dabkowski, *The Age*, 20 September 2004. Available at: http://www.theage.com.au/articles/ 2004/09/19/1095532175865.html?from=moreStories

20 'McCcafe ... Sub-Brand, Para-Sub-Brand Or Co-Brand?' Owen Wright, Professor Lorelle Frazer and Professor Bill Merrilees, Service Industry Research Centre, Griffith University.

21 Azlina Samsudin et al., 'Customer's Perception Towards McDonald's Icon-Based Nutritional Labels', *World Applied Sciences Journal*, 01-07 (2011)

Rule 16 Get your ambition on

1 'Turning point for GAP as 200 stores close worldwide', Harriet Walker, *The Independent*, 13 March 2011.

2 'Retail: Zara bridges Gap to become world's biggest fashion retailer', Graham Keeley and Andrew Clark, *The Guardian*, 12 August 2008.

3 Donald Fisher and Art Twain, *Falling into the Gap*, 2002, Creative Arts Book Company.

4 Louis Nevaer, *Into-and-Out-of-The-Gap*, 2001, Praeger.

5 'The Gap Keeps Running in Place', *Retail Stills*, 2009. Available at: http://retailsails.com/2009/08/20/the-gap-keeps-running-in-place/

6 'J Crew wows New York fashion week', Hadley Freeman, *The Guardian*, 2011. Available at: http://www.guardian.co.uk/fashion/ 2011/sep/13/j-crew-wows-ny-fashion-week

7 'Mickey Drexler: Retail Therapist', Tina Gaudoin, *Wall Street Journal Magazine*, 10 June 2010. Available at; http://magazine.wsj.com/features/the-big-interview/retail-therapist/

8 'Mickey Drexler's Redemption', Meryl Gordon, 21 May 2005, *New York Magazine*. Available at: http://nymag.com/nymetro/news/bizfinance/biz/features/10489/

9 'Paul Pressler's Fall From The Gap', *Business Week*, 26 February 2007. Available at: http://www.businessweek.com/magazine/content/07_09/b4023067.htm

10 'GAP: Decline of a Denim Dynasty', Jennifer Reingold, *Fortune Magazine*, 17 April 2007. Available at: http://money.cnn.com/magazines/fortune/fortune_archive/ 2007/04/30/8405468/index.htm

11 'Print me a Stradivarius', *The Economist*, 10 February 2011.

12 Michael Nielson, *Reinventing Discovery*, 2011, Princeton University Press.

13 Nathaniel Fast, Nir Halevy and Adam Galinksy, 'The destructive nature of power without status', *Journal of Experimental Social Psychology*, Article received 22 July 2011, In Press.

14 Bent Flyvbjerg, Nils Bruzeliusand Werner Rothengatter, *Megaprojects and Risk: An Anatomy of Risk*, 2005, Cambridge University Press.

15 'On a Mission to Sequence the Genomes of 100,000 People', David Ewing Duncan, *The New York Times*, 7 June 2010. Available at: http://www.nytimes.com/2010/06/08/science/08church.html?_r=1

16 'Will we all be tweaking our own genetic code?' Karen Weintraub, 18 September 2011. Available at: http://www.bbc.co.uk/news/technology-14919539

17 'How the Personal Genome Project Could Unlock The Mysteries of Life', Thomas Goetz, *Wired Magazine*, 26 July 2008.
18 'George Church on the Future of Stem Cells, Q&A with the Harvard Geneticist', David Ewing Duncan, 14 September 2011, *Technology Review*, MIT Publications.

Rule 17 Always the beginning

1 'Lego plays hardball with rights to bricks', Ian Austen, *The New York Times*, 3 February 2005. Available at: http://fr.groups.yahoo.com/group/pi_france/message/4376?var=1
2 'The Man Who Would Change Microsoft: Ray Ozzie's Vision for Connection Software', Knowledge@Wharton, 4 April 2007. Available at: http://knowledge.wharton.upenn.edu/article.cfm?articleid=1698
3 'For Lego, an Online Lifeline', Spencer E. Ante, *Bloomberg BusinessWeek*, 23 August 2005.
4 'The Empire Strikes Back', Joanna Pachner, *The Globe and Mail*, 27 May 2009. Available at: http://www.theglobeandmail.com/report-on-business/rob-magazine/the-empire-strikes-back/article1149686/
5 'Tata Motor presents 42% year-on-year sales growth, stuns all', Shishir Asthana, DNA.com, 18 October 2011.
6 Peter Cappelli, Harbir Singh and Michael Useem, 'The Indian Way: Lessons for the US', *The Academy of Management Perspectives*, Volume 24, Number 2, May 2010.
7 'Think before you swallow', Rahul Oberoi, *Business Today*, May 2011. Available at: http://businesstoday.intoday.in/story/mergers-and-acquisitions-throw-up-attractive-investment-options/1/14940.html
8 'JLR better valued than Tata Motors. So why not demerge the two?' Reuters, 29 September 2011. Available at: http://www.firstpost.com/business/jlr-better-valued-than-tata-motors-so-why-not-demerge-the-two-95857.html
9 'Tata Motor's Nano: It's real... so how did they do it?' Justin Fogarty, *Supply Excellence*, 24 March 2009. Available at: http://www.supplyexcellence.com/blog/2009/03/24/tata-motors-nano-its-realso-how-did-they-do-it/

10 'Rata Tata says inspiration for Nano was safety', Daniel Aloi, Chronicle Online, 16 March 2011, Cornell University. Available at: http://www.news.cornell.edu/stories/March11/ NanoSympCover.html

11 'Why a gold-plated Nano will do little for Tata's failing car', R Jagannathan, *Firstpost: Business*, 20 September 2011. Available at: http://www.firstpost.com/business/why-a-gold-plated-nano-will-do-little-for-tatas-failing-car-87924.html

12 'Learning from Tata's Nano Mistakes', Matt Eyring, HBR Blog Network, 11 January 2011. Available at: http://blogs.hbr.org/cs/ 2011/01/learning_from_tatas_nano_mista.html

13 'India Automotive 2010: The Next Giant From Asia', J.D. Power, 15 June 2011. Available at: http://www.tata.com/ article.aspx?artid=ieF78S04XH4=

14 'When creating the Nano, we didn't fear failure: Girish Wagh', Hormazd Sorabjee, DNA.com, 19 October 2010. Available at: http://www.dnaindia.com/money/interview_when-creating-the-nano-we-didnt-fear-failure-girish-wagh_1454655

15 'Resilience and Human Adaptability: Who Rises Above Adversity', Susan B. Fine, 1990 Eleanor Clarke Slagle Lecture, The American Occupational Therapy Association.

16 C. Folke, S.R. Carpenter, B. Walker, M. Scheffer, T. Chapin and J. Rockström, 'Resilience thinking: integrating resilience, adaptability and transformability', *Ecology and Society*, 2010, 15(4): 20.

17 Andy Pike, Stuart Dawley and John Tomaney, 'Resilience, Adaptation and Adaptability', *Cambridge J Regions Econ Soc*, 2010, 3 (1): 59–70.

18 Nancy Scheper-Hughes, 'A Talent for Life: Reflections on Human Vulnerability and Resilience', *Ethnos*, vol. 73:1, March 2008 (pp. 25–56).

Index

Activision   125–26
  Nazi-Zombie game   125–27,
    130
adaptability
  ants and   39–42
  choice and   6
  crisis and   8–9
  desire to do better   186
  distractions   184
  enabling   20
  enthusiasm   192
  imagining future situations
    5, 95–96
  jugaad   191
  minority opinion and   35
  organizational culture   133
  outcomes   5–6
  pace of change   97
  plan B   89–100
  problem solving   29–30
  rebellion and   30–32, 37
  reasons for failing   18, 19–25
  recognizing the need   11–78,
    193
  science and   72
  stability and   67
  three steps   4
  time to adapt   18
  understand the required
    adaptation   79–131, 194
  unintended consequences   91
Adbusters   157
Advanced Cell Technologies
  (ACT)   107
Afghanistan   17, 134
Air India   188

Ajax football team   149–50,
  151, 152
Alonso, Frederic   47
Amazon.com   73, 77, 87
  Kindle   78
ambition   167, 174
Anonymous   144–46, 157
Anonymous Iran   145
ANC (African National
  Congress)   61, 62
ants   39–42
  climatists   41
  competitors   42
  opportunists   41
  time and adaptability   40
Apple   78, 86–87, 115, 118,
  124, 130, 136, 185
  app store   185–86
  iPhone   115, 117
  learning from failure   87
  MobileMe   87
Arafat, President   57
Aristophanes   111
Assange, Julian   145
Aumann, Robert   57
Australia   162
Axelrod, Robert   62

Bach-y-Rita, George   70
Bach-y-Rita, Paul   71–72, 78
Bach-y-Rita, Pedro   69–71
Baez, John   177
Balsille, Jim   114, 116, 117, 118
Barcelona football club   151,
  152
Barnes & Noble (B&N)   74, 77

Barnes, William   73
Battle of the Bulge   86
Beane, Billy   147, 148
Bell, Charlie   162
Bellotti, Mike   148
Berners-Lee, Tim   73
Bertrand, Marc   182
Bertrand Rita   182
Bertrand, Victor   182
Bezos, Jeff   73, 77
Blackberry   114–18, 124
Blériot, Louis   188
Blockbuster   98–99
BMW   83–84, 186
Bono   127
Borders   73–78
Borders, Lewis   74
Borders, Tom   74
Borel, Émile   53
Botha, Pieter Willem   58, 62
Brazil   36
British Airways   49
Bronfman, Edgar   69
Brown, Ann   161
Bush, President George W.   14
Butement, William   86

Calderón, President   35
Camp David Settlement   57
Canada   157
Canas, Vitalino   36
Cantalupo, Jim   162
Chiara, Carl   29–30
Chick, Bill   106
China   156, 175
   'walks'   156
Chrysler   23
Church, George   178
Clinton, President Bill   57
Clyde shipyards 'work-in'
   159–60
collapse   5
collective thinking   121, 123
Compaq   135, 136
Cook, David   99

coping   5
Coulthard, David   44
crisis   8–9
critical thinking   95
Cruyff, Johan   150, 151
curiosity   12

Daewoo   187
Damon, Matt   29
de Klerk, FW   62, 63
decision-making   120–23
   communication and   122
deep adaptation   44, 80, 121,
   149
Denny, Mike   127
Diamond, Jared   2
DiRomualdo, Robert   73, 74
Dish Network   99
diversity   32
Doern, John   69
Donald, Jim   102–04
Drexler, Mickey   169–70, 171,
   172, 173
Durkheim, Emile   32
Dutrou-Bonier, Jean-Baptiste
   94–95

Easter Islanders   91–95
Edwards, Michael   78
Egypt   157
Einstein, Albert   66
Eisenhower, General Dwight   86
empathy   67
emergent thinking   157
entrepreneurs   102
evolution   164, 194
experimentation   85, 175
   mass   177

Facebook   101, 146
failure
   learning from   81, 85,
   164–65
Ferrari   45, 48
Fields, Mark   21

Filettino   27–28, 33
Fiorina, Carly   136
Fisher, Donald   169, 171, 172, 173
Fisher, Doris   169
Fisher, Bob   169
flash mobs   160–61
flash robs   161
Ford   20–21, 22, 25, 43, 186
  resurgence   24–25
Ford, Bill   21
forgiveness   63, 64
Formula One (F1)   42–48
forward thinking   121–22

game theory   53–55
  decision-making   120–22
  forgiveness and   64
  give and take   64
  military strategy and   55
  problem games   66–67
  quantum   65–66
  rules   63
  see also prisoner's dilemma
Gap   167–72
Gates, Bill   174
Gbowee, Leymah   112, 113
GM (General Motors)   22–23, 186
Google   49, 124, 138
Greenberg, Jack   162
Grübel, Oswald   51–52
Gutenberg, Johannes   175

H & M   168
Hamilton, Lewis   45, 47
Hansen, Marka   167–68
Harford, Tim   17
Hasbro   184
Hastings, Reed   98
Heath, Edward   160
Hedström, Peter   113–14
Heyerdahl, Thor   95
hierarchy   141–46
Hitler, Adolf   85

Hong Kong   153
  shanty towns   155–56
Horner, Christian   43, 44, 45, 47
Hotz, George   142–44
HP   135–37
Hudson, Liam   108
Hughes, Nick   118
Huizenga, Wayne   99
human genome   178–79
Huntington, Samuel   61
Hwa, Tung Chee   156
Hydra, the   13

IBM   12
imagination   95–96, 194, 195
Inditex   168, 169, 171, 172
innovation   10
innovators   102
International Monetary Fund   189
internet, the   176
Iraq   134
Issigonis, Sir Alec   82
Italian village mergers   27–28

Jaguar Land Rover (JLR)   186, 191
James, William   71
J-Crew   171
Jobs, Steve   86–87
Josefowicz, Greg   77
jugaad   191

Ka-Shing, Li   153–54
Kenya   112
  mobile banking   118–20
Kmart Corporation   73, 74
Knight, Phil   148
Knorski, Jerzy   71
Kohatsu, Shane   139
Kuhn, Thomas   72
  Philopsophy of Science   174

Lanza, Robert   105–07, 108
Lazardis, Mike   114–16, 118

learning 81–88
Lebow, Bennet S. 78
Lego 182–84, 185
Lewis, Michael 147
Levi Strauss & Co 28–30, 33
Liberia 112, 124
Licence Raj, the 188
Limbaugh, Rush 23–24
Lloyd Webber, Andrew 128
Lonie, Susie 119
Lysistrata 111

maladaptation 91
Mandela, Nelson 61, 63, 67
Marshall, Rob 48
Marshall, Ron 78
mass protest/participation *see*
   swarming
McCord, Jason 125
McDonalds 8, 9, 161–63
   'Plan to Win' 163
McLaren 45, 47
McNamara, Robert 69
Mega Bloks 182–83, 184–85
Mexico 35
Meyer, David 65–66
Michels, Rinus 150, 151
Microsoft 49, 137–38
Migram, Stanley 30–32
Mini car 82–84
mobile phones 160
Moscovici, Serge 35–36
motor racing *see* Formula One
   (F1)
M-Pesa 119
Mubarak, President 157
Mullally, Alan 25
Murphy, Glenn 171–72

National Defense University 14
National Football League
   (NFL) 89
Nelson, Ed 176–77
Nehru, Jawaharlal 188
Netflix 8, 96–100

neural plasticity 71
Newey, Adrian 44, 46, 48
Nike 134, 138, 148–49
Nixon, President Richard 34
Noble, G. Clifford 73
Northern Ireland 113

Oakland Athletics 147–48, 151
Occupy movement 157–58

P & G 28
Page, Patrick 130
Palestinian-Israeli conflict
   56–58, 66, 67
paradigm shift 72
Parker, Sean 101, 107
Pauling, Linus 173–74
peace studies 63
Peano axioms 177
Peano, Guiseppe 177
PepsiCo 81–82
Pfeffer, Philip 78
Piquet Jr, Nelson 47
Pitt, Brad 147
Ponoko 174–75
Portugal 33–34
   drug policy 33–34, 36
Pounding, Lieutenant Colonel
   Jeffrey E 164
power 172–73
Pressler, Paul 170–71
printing 175–76
prisoner's dilemma, the 54,
   62–63
Prodromou, Peter 48
proximity fuse 86
Pull & Bear 167, 168

quantum game theory 65–66

radical thinkers 101–09
   convergents/divergents 108
Ralph Lauren 169
Rapa Nui *see* Easter Islanders
Rapoport, Anatol 63

Red Bull   43–48, 130
Reid, Jimmy   160
Renaissance, the   176
Research in Motion (RIM)
   114–18
resilience   130
Reynolds, Jack   149–50, 151
Riggio, Leonard   73–74
Ritvik   182
Rohner, Marcel   52
Rometty, Virginia   12
Rooney Rule, the   89–90, 100
Rover Group   83–84
rules of adaptability   1

sabermetrics   147
Safaricom   119
Sagentia   119
Sauer Commission   59
Schelling, Thomas   55
Schultz, Howard   102, 107
science of adaptability   2
Sellari, Luca   27
'sex strikes'   111–12
shallow adaptation   80, 121
Shakespeare, Willian   53
Shectman, Danny   173–74
Sirleaf, Ellen Johnson   112
Skinner, Jim   162–63
smart mobs   161
Smut, Jan   59
Snyder, Jessie   125–27, 130
social media   28
Sony   9, 78, 141–44
South Africa   67, 113
   apartheid and   58–62
Spiderman   127–30
St Paul's cathedral protest
   158–59
Starbucks   8, 102–04
Star Trek   65
Strauss, Ofra   69
'strike of crossed legs'   112
Stringer, Sir Howard   141
super-adaptation   84

survival   9, 182, 195
swarming   16, 157–58, 160, 165
swerving   157, 160, 165

Tao, Terry   177
Tata, Jamsetji   187–88, 189
Tata, JRD   188
Tata Motors   186–92
   acquisition strategy   187
   Nano, the   190–92
Tata, Ratan   189, 192
Taylor, Charles   112
Taymor, Julie   127, 128
thriving   5
tiki-taka   151
Toyota   21–22, 23, 25, 44
   approach to adaptation   22
   Prius   22, 23, 190
transcendence   6
Treyarch   125
Tropicana   81–82, 85
Twitter   69, 157, 197
Twitter Revolution   161
Tyco   182

Ullman, Harlan   14
University of Oregon football
   team   148, 151, 152
University of Ottawa   123
University of Southern
   California   172
University of Virginia   120
UBS   51–52, 66, 67
UPS   19
USPS (US Postal Service)   19
USA
   budgetary crisis (2011)   123
   drug policy   34–35
US military   14, 164
   Iraq war   14–17
   'shock and awe'   14
   strategy   55

Van Horne, Todd   149
Vettel, Sebastian   46

Viacom   99
video streaming   96
Viejo, Raimundo   157
Vietnam war   17, 69
Villiger, Kaspar   52
Virgin   49
Vodafone   118, 119
Von Neumann, John   54, 58

Wade, James   14
Wagh, Grish   192
Waldenbooks   76, 77

Warner Music   69
Webber, Mark   44
Whitman, Meg   137
wikileaks   145
winning   55, 191, 195
woodblock printing   175
World Design Impact Prize   190
World Wide Web   73, 177

zero-sum games   54 *see also*
    game theory
Zuckerberg, Mark   101